PIZZA AND PASTA

PIZZA
— AND —
PASTA

SUSAN CONTE

TREASURE PRESS

ACKNOWLEDGEMENTS

The author would like to thank all her friends and relations who helped in the preparation of the book, but in particular:

Dott, Mario Nervegna, Managing Director of Voiello Pasta, Naples, for his valuable information about pasta.

Cathy Biondi for her collaboration on homemade egg pasta.

Manlio Conte her husband, for his useful criticism and suggestions while testing new recipes.

First published in Great Britain in 1986 by
Hamlyn Publishing

This edition published in 1988 by
Treasure Press
Michelin House
81 Fulham Road
London SW3 6RB

Reprinted 1989

ISBN 1 85051 291 4

Printed in Hungary

The author and publishers would like to thank Elizabeth David Ltd, 46 Bourne Street, London SW1, for lending the kitchen equipment shown in the photograph on page 23.
Inside photography by Vernon Morgan
Line drawings by Sally Grover

CONTENTS

USEFUL FACTS AND FIGURES

NOTES ON METRICATION

In this book quantities are given in metric and Imperial measures. Exact conversion from Imperial to metric measures does not usually give very convenient working quantities and so the metric measures have been rounded off into units of 25 grams. The table below shows the recommended equivalents.

Ounces	Approx g to nearest whole figure	Recommended conversion to nearest unit of 25
1	28	25
2	57	50
3	85	75
4	113	100
5	142	150
6	170	175
7	198	200
8	227	225
9	255	250
10	283	275
11	312	300
12	340	350
13	368	375
14	396	400
15	425	425
16 (1 lb)	454	450

Note: When converting quantities over 16 oz first add the appropriate figures in the centre column, then adjust to the nearest unit of 25. As a general guide, 1 kg (1000 g) equals 2.2 lb or about 2 lb 3 oz. This method of conversion gives good results in nearly all cases, although in certain pastry and cake recipes a more accurate conversion is necessary to produce a balanced recipe.

Liquid measures The millilitre has been used in this book and the following table gives a few examples.

Imperial	Approx ml to nearest whole figure	Recommended ml
$\frac{1}{4}$ pint	142	150 ml
$\frac{1}{2}$ pint	283	300 ml
$\frac{3}{4}$ pint	425	450 ml
1 pint	567	600 ml
$1\frac{1}{2}$ pints	851	900 ml
$1\frac{3}{4}$ pints	992	1000 ml (1 litre)

Spoon measures All spoon measures given in this book are level unless otherwise stated.

Can sizes At present, cans are marked with the exact (usually to the nearest whole number) metric equivalent of the Imperial weight of the contents, so we have followed this practice when giving can sizes.

Oven temperatures The table below gives recommended equivalents.

	°C	°F	Gas Mark
Very cool	110	225	$\frac{1}{4}$
	120	250	$\frac{1}{2}$
Cool	140	275	1
	150	300	2
Moderate	160	325	3
	180	350	4
Moderately hot	190	375	5
	200	400	6
Hot	220	425	7
	230	450	8
Very Hot	240	475	9

NOTES FOR AMERICAN AND AUSTRALIAN USERS

In America the 8-fl oz measuring cup is used. In Australia metric measures are now used in conjunction with the standard 250-ml measuring cup. The Imperial pint, used in Britain and Australia, is 20 fl oz, while the American pint is 16 fl oz. It is important to remember that the Australian tablespoon differs from both the British and American tablespoons; the table below gives a comparison. The British standard tablespoon, which has been used thoughout this book, holds 17.7 ml, the American 14.2 ml, and the Australian 20 ml. A teaspoon holds approximately 5 ml in all three countries.

British	American	Australian
1 teaspoon	1 teaspoon	1 teaspoon
1 tablespoon	1 tablespoon	1 tablespoon
2 tablespoons	3 tablespoons	2 tablespoons
$3\frac{1}{2}$ tablespoons	4 tablespoons	3 tablespoons
4 tablespoons	5 tablespoons	$3\frac{1}{2}$ tablespoons

An Imperial/American guide to solid and liquid measures

Imperial	American
Solid measures	
1 lb butter or margarine	2 cups
1 lb flour	4 cups
1 lb granulated or caster sugar	2 cups
1 lb icing sugar	3 cups
8 oz rice	1 cup
Liquid measures	
$\frac{1}{4}$ pint liquid	$\frac{2}{3}$ cup liquid
$\frac{1}{2}$ pint	$1\frac{1}{4}$ cups
$\frac{3}{4}$ pint	2 cups
1 pint	$2\frac{1}{2}$ cups
$1\frac{1}{2}$ pints	$3\frac{3}{4}$ cups
2 pints	5 cups ($2\frac{1}{2}$ pints)

Note: When making any of the recipes in this book, only follow one set of measures as they are not interchangeable.

FOREWORD

Living abroad for so many years I feel the need every now and then to read an English newspaper or magazine, despite fluency in my adopted language. I am nearly always disappointed when turning to the cookery pages and reading an article on Italian cookery, however, to find that the recipes are 'adapted' to the British way of eating. Italian words are mis-spelt and the recipes are not true to the authentic Italian versions. I am constantly puzzled as to why recipes should be so distorted. Is it because the writer fears that the British are incapable of appreciating anything but ravioli on toast, or soggy, frozen pizza? My personal experience of British taste buds has been to the contrary. Having worked for many years in an English school in Rome I have come into contact with hundreds of expatriates who, like myself, adore Italian food. We even miss it when home in Britain and hardly a visit goes by without making a *spaghettata* for family and friends, which, I may say, is greatly appreciated.

I decided, therefore, to compile this book of authentic Italian recipes – dishes which are served daily in restaurants and in the home – as an introduction to cooking dried pasta and to making pasta and pizzas at home. A multitude of adaptable pasta sauces and pizza toppings follows the recipes for home-made pasta and pizza. The ingredients can be found easily as supermarkets and larger grocery stores are extremely well stocked these days with Italian products or the British equivalent. The dishes, in most cases, satisfy the present day need for something quick and easy to make, yet offer an inviting change from the usual 'fast food' which seems to have taken over everyday meal planning.

I am sure that these Italian recipes will be welcomed not only by those of you who have visited Italy but also by those of you who enjoy experimenting in the kitchen with new ways of cooking and eating. Pasta and pizzas can open up a whole new range of meals for both family and friends and as there are so many sauces and toppings to choose from you never get bored with Italian cooking. Whether vegetarian or carnivore, there are recipes to suit everyone's taste! Do not be afraid to be adventurous once you have mastered the basic principles. The variations are infinite. *Buon Appetito*!

Susan Conte

PASTA

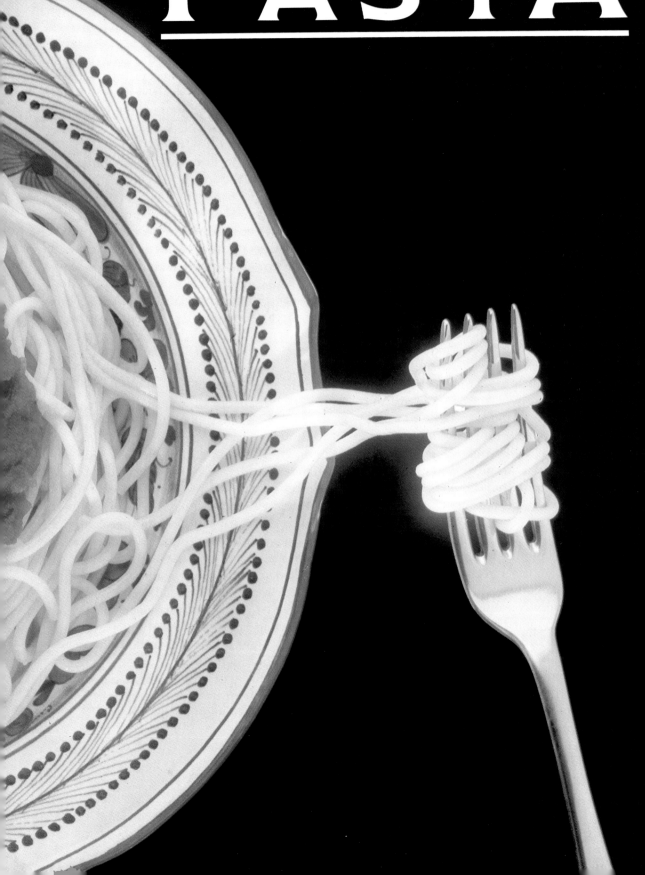

HISTORICAL BACKGROUND

The first known reference to dried pasta can be traced to the Middle Ages in Sicily, when the island was under Arab domination. Some say that the Arabs introduced this foodstuff to Sicily, others say that the name *maccheroni* is derived from the Sicilian word *maccarruni* meaning 'made into a dough by force', and that therefore Sicily is the place of origin. One thing that is certain, however, is that it was not brought to Italy from China by 14th century explorer Marco Polo, as references to dried pasta date from before he had returned from his travels.

The need to dry pasta, which had been eaten freshly made for centuries, came with the increased trading which resulted from the establishment of the Marine Republics in Venice, Genoa, Pisa and Amalfi. A type of foodstuff which would not perish and which could easily be stored on board ship for long voyages needed to be produced. Sailors from Amalfi on their frequent voyages to Sicily took the Sicilian art of drying pasta back home with them. As a result, the region around the Gulf of Naples started to produce its own dried pasta.

However, the special durum wheat necessary for production had to be imported from other regions, such as Sicily or Puglia and consequently the pasta was costly and only consumed by the richer classes. The poorer people continued to eat a diet of vegetables and the Neapolitans were often referred to at the time as 'leaf-eaters'. A famous old Neapolitan proverb cited three things which could bring a household to ruin: cakes, fresh bread and maccheroni. (Fresh bread was regarded as ruinous as it was consumed more rapidly than stale bread!)

The first pasta factories (*pastifici*) appeared around Genoa, the Gulf of Naples and in Sicily, but the two places which continued to thrive, due to either the ideal climate or the good grain production, were Naples and Sicily. Naples had by far the best geographical position, being surrounded on three sides by mountains, situated on the sea and having a mild climate.

The pasta makers in those days had to be expert weather forecasters as well as craftsmen, in order to predict the day's weather and decide whether to produce pasta that day and if so which type. The pasta was made by hand and then dried on terraces. Consequently, the head pasta-maker had to decide to make short or long pasta depending on whether there was hot sun, a warm breeze from the land, or a moist breeze off the sea.

The discovery of electricity in the early 1900s made life much easier for the pasta industry. Machines were invented for mixing the pasta dough and electrically controlled drying chambers were introduced. Pasta production was no longer limited to warm climates and on pressing a button the quantity of pasta that had once taken a month to produce was obtained in an hour.

Today, almost every supermarket offers a large range of pasta and many delicatessens or specialist Italian shops import an enormous variety of pasta shapes. New shapes and sizes are frequently introduced or revived.

Pizza and pasta restaurants are popular in many high streets and the appetite for further editions seems inexhaustible!

HOW PASTA IS MANUFACTURED

Contrary to what the BBC would have liked us to believe on April 1st some years ago, spaghetti does not grow on trees, it is manufactured. The basic ingredient is durum wheat. Up until 1967 pasta could be made from both hard or soft wheat semolina. The soft wheat semolina pasta was cheaper, but obviously far inferior to that made from durum wheat as the pasta easily disintegrated when cooked. A law was then passed which prevented the use of any wheat except durum wheat, but even now you can find different qualities of pasta depending on the quality of the durum wheat used. Good pasta should not become soft and slimy while cooking and should hold its perfectly cooked state *al dente* for up to ten minutes, once drained, before being classed as 'overcooked'.

RAW MATERIALS

Durum wheat is grown in Italy mainly in the central-southern regions. The largest durum wheat production areas are the plain of Puglia, Sicily and the Tuscan Maremma. Durum wheat is also grown in the Mediterranean basin, the Middle East, Russia and the Americas. The main exporting countries are the USA, Canada and Argentina. The best durum wheats are those richest in gluten, which gives the pasta its best cooking qualities. The pasta factories in Italy make their pasta from a mixture of various types of durum wheat, a large proportion of which is usually Candeal wheat from Argentina. One large pasta manufacturer in Naples invested large sums of money in researching the best mutation of several types of wheat to obtain a semolina which is just right for making perfect pasta.

PRODUCTION

The durum wheat is ground into semolina in the mills and then delivered to the pasta factory (*pastificio*) where it is checked for quality and impurities and stored in the storage silos. The semolina is then mixed with the quantity of water needed to obtain a good dough. Mixing takes place in large tubs, the last of which is under vacuum, which contributes to the amber colour of the pasta. The dough is then extruded through various different shapes of nozzles to form the type of pasta being manufactured that day.

There are two types of extruding nozzles, teflon and bronze. The teflon nozzle gives the pasta a smooth, translucent surface, whereas the bronze one gives the pasta a rough, opaque surface. The factories using the teflon nozzles can produce far more pasta in a shorter time than those using the bronze ones, as the dough passes through teflon much more quickly than it does through bronze. One of the oldest pasta factories in Naples, Voiello, still uses the old-fashioned bronze variety, however, as the management is not interested in increased production but in quality; although slower production raises the price, they say that real pasta lovers are willing to pay a little more to get perfect pasta.

There are two points of view over the drying process, too. The teflon users say that with modern technology the drying process can be speeded up (8–11 hours) without detriment to the quality of the pasta. The bronze users, however, say that pasta has to be dried slowly to enable it to ferment slightly and gain flavour (12–48 hours depending on the pasta shape). In both cases, however, the pasta is dried until the humidity has fallen within the legal limits of 12.5 per cent. The pasta is then allowed to mature in the storage silos before being weighed and packaged, after which it is ready for sale. Pasta has a shelf-life of two years provided that it is stored in a cool, dry place away from flour or rice which could contaminate it with weevils.

The experts say that pasta, like wine, improves with age.

PASTA SHAPES

The first pasta shapes to exist were similar to those of the fettuccine and spaghetti families as we know them today. The more elaborate forms evolved with the introduction of sophisticated sauces. They were invented in order to increase the surface area of pasta which could be coated with sauce.

The hole through the centre of bucatini, penne and rigatoni, for example, enables the sauce to enter the pasta as well as to coat it. Gomiti and conchiglie trap the sauce inside the pasta only releasing its full flavour when in the mouth. Eliche, fusilli and farfalle increase appreciation of the sauce by offering a greater surface area for it to rest on. The tubetti family vary in size and are chosen accordingly, depending on whether they are needed to house peas or beans in the pasta soup being prepared.

The pasta industry is constantly bringing out new shapes or reviving old ones. One large Neapolitan pasta manufacturer recently commissioned a famous designer, Giugiaro, to design a totally new pasta shape called *marille*, which was launched with great pride, making front-page news. Two loops attract the maximum amount of sauce. There are over one hundred different forms of pasta on the market in Italy, but here only the most common or the most easily available shapes are mentioned. Many of the short pasta shapes are available in both the smooth and ribbed forms.

AN ABC OF PASTA SHAPES

AGNOLOTTI: Freshly made pasta stuffed with ricotta cheese and spinach. *Origin*: uncertain *Cooking time*: fresh pasta is cooked when it rises to the surface of the boiling water.

ANELLINI (small rings): Very small pasta used in consommé. *Origin*: uncertain *Cooking time*: 5 minutes

BUCATINI: Thick spaghetti with a hole through the centre. *Origin*: Rome *Cooking time*: 9 minutes

CANNELLONI: Large tubular pasta to be filled with meat or vegetable stuffing and baked in the oven. *Origin*: uncertain *Cooking time*: 13 minutes

CAPELLINI (fine hairs): The thinnest form of 'spaghetti'. *Origin*: central, northern Italy *Cooking time*: 4 minutes

CONCHIGLIE (shells): *Origin*: Naples *Cooking time*: 16 minutes

DITALI (thimbles): *Origin*: Naples *Cooking time*: 12 minutes

DITALINI (small thimbles): *Origin*: uncertain *Cooking time*: 8 minutes

ELICHE (propellers): *Origin*: northern Italy *Cooking time*: 12 minutes

FARFALLE (Butterflies or Bow ties): Butterflies herald the coming of spring and are therefore served with summer sauces. *Origin*: northern Italy *Cooking time*: 12 minutes

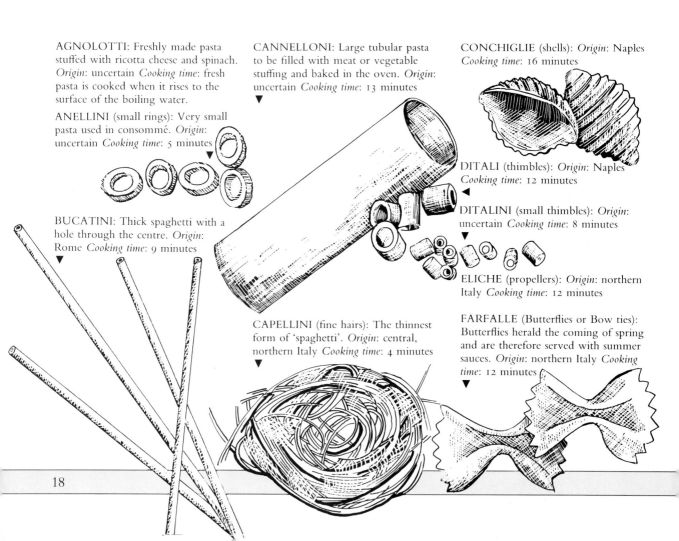

FETTUCCINE (thin ribbons): Egg pasta, often freshly made. Manufactured in the form of nests which come loose in boiling water. *Origin*: central, northern Italy *Cooking time*: 7 minutes ▼

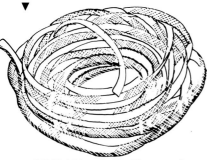

FUSILLI (thin spirals): These can be either long or short. They were originally made by wrapping a length of spaghetti around a knitting needle. *Origin*: long – Naples; short – central, northern Italy *Cooking time*: 17 minutes – long, 15 minutes – short ▼

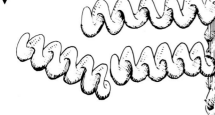

GNOCCHI: Large gnocchi-shaped pasta. *Origin*: Naples *Cooking time*: 15 minutes. ▼

GNOCCHETTI ALLA SARDA: Small gnocchi-shaped pasta. *Origin*: Sardinia *Cooking time*: 15 minutes

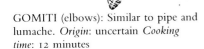

GOMITI (elbows): Similar to pipe and lumache. *Origin*: uncertain *Cooking time*: 12 minutes

LANCETTE (small spears): Very small pasta shapes used in consommé. *Origin*: uncertain *Cooking time*: 7 minutes

LASAGNE: Wide strips of pasta used for baking. They can be either white or green and with or without a frilly edge. The green colouring is obtained by adding spinach to the pasta dough. *Origin*: flat – Naples, frilly – central, southern Italy *Cooking time*: flat – 7 minutes, frilly – 20 minutes ▼

LINGUINE (small tongues): Flat 'spaghetti', *Origin*: Genoa *Cooking time*: 11 minutes

LUMACHE (snails): The giant-sized ones are stuffed and baked in the oven. The smaller ones are served with sauces. Similar to gomiti and pipe. *Origin*: Naples *Cooking time*: 12 minutes ▼

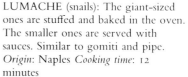

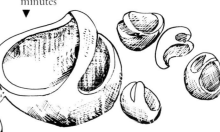

MAFALDINE: Widish ribbons of pasta with frilly edges. This pasta is named after Princess Mafalda of Savoy as it is similar in appearance to the trimmings she used on her dresses. *Origin*: central, northern Italy *Cooking time*: 7 minutes

MEZZE MANICHE (short sleeves): Short, tubular pasta. As its name implies it is meant to be served with summer sauces. *Origin*: Naples *Cooking time*: 10 minutes ▼

MISTA (PASTA) (mixed pasta): Originally sold by grocers as leftovers from the bottom of the various jars of pasta shapes. Now produced industrially as mixed pasta. *Origin*: Naples *Cooking time*: 9 minutes

OCCHI DI LUPO (wolves' eyes): Small, tubular pasta similar to ditali. *Origin*: uncertain *Cooking time*: 12 minutes

ORECCHIETTE (small ears): The farmers' wives who make these by hand from an old recipe still cannot agree as to whose ears these are meant to represent! This pasta is now also made industrially. *Origin*: Puglia *Cooking time*: 15 minutes

PAGLIA E FIENO (straw and hay): Thin green and white ribbons of pasta usually freshly made. The green colour is obtained by adding spinach to the pasta dough. Similar to fettuccine. *Cooking time*: fresh pasta is cooked when it rises to the surface of the boiling water.

PENNE (quills): *Origin*: Naples *Cooking time*: 12 minutes
▼

PENNETTE (small quills): *Origin*: Naples *Cooking time*: 10 minutes

PEPE (pepper): Tiny cuboid grains of pasta used in consommé. *Origin*: Naples *Cooking time*: 12 minutes

PERCIATELLI: Very thick 'spaghetti' with a hole through the centre. Thicker than bucatini. *Origin*: Naples *Cooking time*: 8 minutes

PIPE (pipes): Similar to lumache and gomiti both in shape and size. *Origin*: central, northern Italy *Cooking time*: 12 minutes
▼

QUADRETTI (small squares): Small squares of egg pasta used in consommé. *Cooking time*: 5 minutes

RAVIOLI: Square-shaped fresh pasta filled with meat and spices, or ricotta cheese and spinach. *Origin*: central, northern Italy *Cooking time*: similar to other freshly cooked pasta.
▼

RIGATONI (large ribbed ones): Short, tubular pasta which is always ribbed. This pasta is a fundamental ingredient of Roman cuisine. It can be served with almost any type of sauce. *Origin*: Rome *Cooking time*: 16 minutes
▼

SEDANI (celery stalks): These are thinner than rigatoni and are very slightly curved. *Origin*: Naples *Cooking time*: 15 minutes

SPAGHETTI (thin strings): The name 'spaghetti' tends to cover all the long, thin pasta forms from capellini to vermicelli, without taking into consideration their real thickness. Real spaghetti, however, comes between capellini and vermicelli. *Origin*: central, northern Italy *Cooking time*: 8 minutes ▼

STELLINE (small stars): Small pasta shape used in consommé. *Origin*: uncertain *Cooking time*: 7 minutes ▶

TAGLIATELLE: Similar to fettuccine but slightly thinner. Like fettuccine it is always manufactured in a nest shape which comes loose during the cooking. *Origin*: central, northern Italy *Cooking time*: 6 minutes

TAGLIOLINI: Egg pasta similar to fettuccine and tagliatelle but thinner than the other two. *Origin*: central, northern Italy *Cooking time*: 5 minutes

TORTELLINI: Freshly made pasta stuffed with a filling made from Parma ham, veal, egg and spices. *Origin*: Bologna, Emilia-Romagna *Cooking time*: it is cooked when it rises to the surface of the boiling water.
▼

TORTIGLIONI (large twisted ones): Similar to rigatoni but are slightly curved and twisted. *Origin*: Naples *Cooking time*: 16 minutes
▼

TRENETTE: Similar to linguine but slightly thinner. *Origin*: Naples *Cooking time*: 7 minutes

TUBETTI (small tubes): Similar to ditali. *Origin*: Naples *Cooking time*: 12 minutes

VERMICELLI (thin worms): The thickest of the 'spaghetti' family and often, mistakenly, called spaghetti. *Origin*: central, northern Italy *Cooking time*: 10 minutes

ZITI (spinsters): The name *zita* in Neapolitan means a young woman who is about to get married. This pasta is named after these 'spinsters of the parish', as it was traditionally served at their wedding feast. A long form of macaroni, ziti have to be broken into shorter lengths before cooking. *Origin*: Naples *Cooking time*: 11 minutes
▼

SUITABLE SAUCES FOR PASTA SHAPES

PASTA	SIMPLE SAUCES		COMPLEX SAUCES USING –				SOUPS	
	Oil and/or tomato	Butter	Cheese/Cream	Meat	Fish/Seafood	Vegetables	Consommé	Thick soups
Agnolotti		√		√√				
Anellini							√√	
Bucatini			Amatriciana					
Cannelloni	√			√√				
Capellini	√						√√	
Conchiglie	√√			√				
Ditali	√	√						√√
Ditalini	√							√√
Eliche	√		√	√√		√		
Farfalle	√√	√	√					
Fettuccine		√	√√	√				
Fusilli				√√				
Gnocchi	√							
Gnocchetti Sardi	√		√	√				√√
Gomiti	√		√	√				
Lancette							√√	
Lasagne				√√				
Linguine	√√	√			√√			
Lumache	√		√	√				
Mafaldine			√	√		√		
Mezze Maniche	√							
Mista (Pasta)								√√
Occhi di Lupo	√	√						√√
Orecchiette				√		√√		
Paglia e Fieno		√	√√	√				
Penne	√√		√	√				
Pennette	√√		√	√				
Pepe							√√	
Perciatelli				√√				
Pipe	√		√	√				
Quadretti							√√	
Ravioli		√√	√	√√				
Rigatoni	√		√	√√		√		
Sedani			√	√				
Spaghetti	√√	√			√√			
Stelline							√√	
Tagliatelle		√	√√	√				
Tagliolini		√	√√	√				
Tortellini		√	√√	√			√	
Tortiglioni				√√		√		
Trenette	Pesto	√			√			
Tubetti	√							√√
Vermicelli	√	√			√√			
Ziti				Ragoût				

√ **suitable**   √√ **ideal**

HOW TO COOK DRIED PASTA

BASIC EQUIPMENT

1 Three-quarters fill with water a pan large enough to allow the pasta to swell and to be stirred frequently. If you are cooking spaghetti or other long pasta, use a tall pan to avoid burning the ends of the pasta while waiting for it to sink into the boiling water. (Many British recipes recommend the addition of oil to the water to prevent the pasta from sticking together. If you follow the method correctly this is not necessary. I have never yet met an Italian who adds oil to the cooking water!)

2 Bring the water to a fast boil.

3 Add about 1 generous tablespoon of salt to 4 litres/7 pints of water. Remember that the amount of salt used is in proportion to the volume of water and not to the quantity of pasta.

4 Drop in the pasta, bringing the water back to a fast boil immediately.

5 Using a wooden spatula, or in the case of long pasta a cooking fork, stir frequently to prevent the pasta from sticking to itself or the pan.

6 Two or three minutes before the end of the recommended cooking time, test the pasta. The pasta is perfectly cooked when the uncooked core in the centre is just about to disappear or, in the case of spaghetti, when you can squeeze it between thumb and forefinger to break it. Italians always eat pasta *al dente* which means 'resistant to the tooth'.

7 Take the pan off the boil and add a drop of cold tap water to prevent the pasta from overcooking.

8 Drain the pasta well through a colander.

9 Serve immediately with an appropriate sauce.

10 Buon Appetito!

If you are a pasta fanatic, or are thinking of becoming one, it is a good idea to buy yourself a set of basic equipment should you not possess utensils similar to those illustrated already. The pans described here are ideal for preparing pasta for four people.

1 **A tall pan**, about 18 cm/7 in high and 18 cm/7 in. in diameter. This is absolutely essential when cooking spaghetti or other long pasta, so that the pasta can descend slowly into the boiling water without the ends burning over the sides of the pan.

2 **A flameproof earthenware casserole**, about 25 cm/10 in. in diameter and suitable for using on the hob. This is used for making certain slow-cooking sauces and really does give them a better flavour. A pressure cooker *can* be used to speed up the process.

3 **A large saucepan**, approximately 18 cm/7 in. in diameter, is used for most soups and some sauces.

4 **A large frying pan**, approximately 25 cm/10 in. in diameter, is used for sauces which need to lose steam quickly and to 'fry' as opposed to 'boil'.

5 **A large ladle** is used for serving the sauces and mixing and serving short pasta shapes and soups.

6 **A large, two-pronged cooking fork** is needed for cooking, mixing and serving spaghetti and other long pasta.

7 **A wooden spoon** is used for making sauces and soups.

8 **A chopping knife, or mezzaluna**, is needed for preparing the ingredients for some sauces.

9 **Spaghetti tongs** are extremely useful for beginners for serving long pasta.

HOME-MADE PASTA

It is much easier than you might think to make pasta at home. Once you have acquired the knack of kneading the dough and got used to the length of the rolling pin, you can make pasta in less than half an hour. Obviously, if you have a pasta machine, even if it is one which only rolls out the dough and cuts it, then your work load will be considerably lighter.

Recipes for pasta dough vary considerably, but the general rule is 1 egg and 100 g/4 oz of plain flour per person. Some recipes add oil, others substitute one of the eggs with water, but the recipes and methods I have given in this book were taught to me by a friend of mine from Emilia-Romagna. She has been making pasta at home since she was a small child and Emilia-Romagna is the 'home' of home-made egg pasta.

Unless you are the proud owner of an automatic pasta maker you will need a few pieces of basic equipment should you wish to embark on the very worthwhile task of making your own pasta.

1   A large, flat working surface in marble, wood or formica, which should be open on at least three sides, or you will have difficulty managing the long rolling pin.

2   A long, wooden rolling pin (at least 70 cm/ 28 in). It has to be longer than usual to roll out the circles of pasta to the required diameter, so do not try and make do with the one you already have!

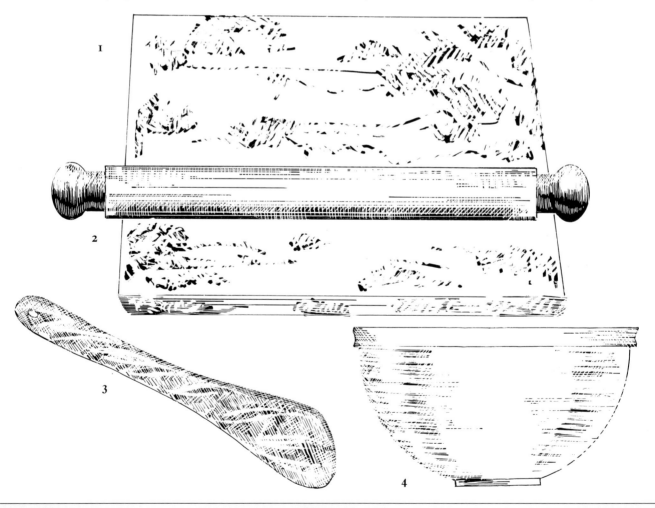

3 **A scraper or blunt knife** for scraping the table as you are mixing the dough.

4 **A small bowl** used for covering the dough while it is resting.

5 **A warm tea-towel** for drying the dough when making fettuccine.

6 **A sharp, heavy chopping knife** for cutting the fettuccine.

7 **A pastry wheel** for cutting ravioli.

8 **A pastry cutter** for cutting agnolotti.

9 **A large tray or two large, oval plates** for laying out the pasta when it is ready.

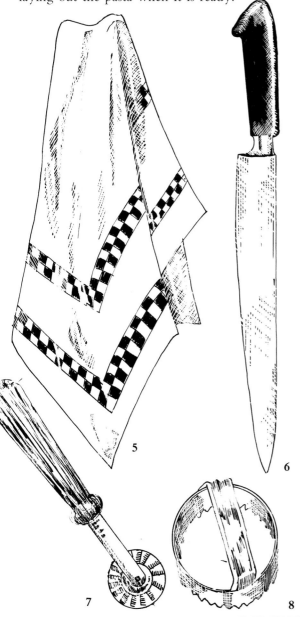

Shapes That Can be Cut from Fresh, Home-made Egg Pasta

Fettuccine: thin ribbons of pasta approximately 6–7 mm/$\frac{3}{8}$ in wide.

Tagliatelle: thin ribbons of pasta approximately 5 mm/$\frac{1}{4}$ in wide.

Tagliolini: thin ribbons of pasta approximately 3 mm/$\frac{1}{8}$ in wide.

Paglia e Fieno (straw and hay): similar to tagliatelle but some are made from plain pasta (the straw) and others from green pasta (the hay).

Pappardelle: wider ribbons of pasta about 2.5 cm/1 in wide and often cut with fluted edges.

Lasagne Napoletane: long, wide strips of pasta about 5 cm/2 in wide and up to 40 cm/16 in long.

Lasagne: rectangles of pasta approximately 10 × 15 cm/4 × 6 in.

Cannelloni: squares of pasta about 10 × 10 cm/4 × 4 in, which are then made into rolls.

Farfalle: rectangles of pasta approximately 5 × 2.5 cm/2 × 1 in, cut with a fluted edge and then pinched up in the middle to form a 'butterfly'!

Quadrucci: tiny squares of pasta approximately 7 × 7 mm/$\frac{3}{8}$ × $\frac{3}{8}$ in which can be cut from the pieces of pasta left over after cutting out the other shapes.

Stuffed pasta **Tortellini, Agnolotti, Ravioli**

MAKING FETTUCCINE

1   Heap the flour on to a work surface, make a well in the centre, and break in the eggs. Using a fork, lightly beat the eggs and gradually incorporate the flour from the inside out.

2   Continue with your hands until you have a soft dough. Knead the dough, using the heel of your palms to work it into a roll. Fold in the ends and start again. Leave the dough to rest.

3   Knead the dough into a roll again and twist it into two equal pieces. Knead one piece into a ball. Using a long rolling pin, roll out the dough away from you, ensuring the edges of the circle are as thin as the centre.

4   Keep rolling out until the dough is extremely thin and almost transparent. Place a warm tea-towel over the circle of dough and roll them together round the rolling pin. Leave for 5 minutes, then unroll the pasta.

5   Roll up the circle of pasta in stages into the centre, making each roll about 5 cm/2 in across. Place near the edge of the work surface and, using a very sharp knife, cut the pasta into 5-mm–1-cm/$\frac{1}{4}$–$\frac{1}{2}$ in strips.

6   Slide the blade of the knife under each strip, lift up the knife, and the fettuccine will unfold down each side of the blade.

Fettuccine

Illustrated on pages 26 and 27

**about 500 g/18 oz strong plain flour plus
flour for working
5 medium eggs**

Heap the flour on to a flat working surface and make a deep well in the centre. Break the eggs into the well. Using a fork, lightly beat the eggs and gradually start incorporating the flour taking it from the bottom inside of the well.

Continue incorporating the flour into the eggs with the fork, taking care not to break the sides of the well or the eggs will escape, until you have a thickish mixture. Continue with your hands, working from the inside outwards until you have a soft dough and all the flour has been incorporated. While working the flour into the egg keep scraping the working surface and rubbing your hands with flour so that all the mixture that has stuck to your hands or the table can be rubbed off and incorporated into the dough. When the dough is ready the table should be clean!

Knead the dough for about 10 minutes, using the heel of your palms and a rhythmic peddling movement to work the dough into a roll, fold in the ends and start again. The finished dough should be smooth and fairly firm to the touch.

Leave the dough to rest for 5–6 minutes, covering it with a bowl to prevent the surface from drying out.

Knead the dough once more into a roll and twist it into two equal pieces. Put one piece back under the bowl and knead the other into a ball.

Using a long rolling pin, roll out the dough, sprinkling it with a little flour when necessary to prevent sticking and turning it by rolling it around the rolling pin. As the dough increases in diameter, part of the circle should hang over the edge of the working surface nearest to you and you should be rolling away from you, making sure that the edges of the circle are as thin as the centre. Keep rolling out until the dough is extremely thin and almost transparent. For the quantities given in this recipe, each rolled out circle should be between 60–65 cm/24–26 in. in diameter.

Place a warm tea-towel over the circle of dough and roll them together around the rolling pin. Leave for approximately 5 minutes, then unroll the pasta so that it is lying on top of the tea-towel.

Allow it to stand and finish drying for another 5–10 minutes, depending on the heat and humidity of the kitchen and the weather. When ready the pasta should feel dry to the touch.

Roll up the circle of pasta starting from opposite sides of the circle into the centre, each 'roll' being about 5 cm/2 in across. Place the rolls near the edge of the working surface nearest to you and using a very sharp, heavy chopping knife, cut the pasta into strips measuring from 5 mm–1 cm/$\frac{1}{4}$–$\frac{1}{2}$ in, depending on individual preference. Slide the blade of the knife under the cut pasta up to the halfway point and lift up the knife. The fettuccine will unfold down each side of the blade. Take the fettuccine off the knife by collecting them up with your fingers. Lay them, folded in two, on a large plate. Repeat the rolling and cutting process with the other half of the dough.

Freshly made pasta needs a larger quantity of water than dried pasta. Drop the pasta into the salted water when it is boiling fast. Use two wooden cooking forks to lift and separate the pasta occasionally to prevent it from sticking. When the water comes back to boiling point leave the pasta to cook for a further 2–3 minutes, then lift it out of the water using the cooking forks. Drain the pasta well in the colander before putting it in a serving dish and mixing it with the sauce. Never pour the pasta out of the pan directly into the serving dish as it will get so ravelled that it is impossible to serve.

Serve immediately with your favourite sauce.

Sauce choice butter, Bolognese, cream sauces

Cook's Tips

1 Metal utensils should be used as little as possible while making and cooking fresh pasta.
2 The thickness of the pasta dough before cutting depends on how you intend to serve it. It should be very thin for butter sauce, slightly thicker for cream sauces and slightly thicker still for meat and tomato sauces.
3 Never attempt to make pasta at home unless you are in the mood.
4 'La bravura della cuoca si vede dalla lunghezza delle sue fettuccine'. The cleverness of the cook can be seen in the length of her fettuccine: an old Emilian proverb!
5 Fettuccine are best made and served the same day, but can be kept in the refrigerator for 24 hours or frozen. Cook frozen pasta while still frozen or it will become soggy while thawing out.

GREEN PASTA

300 g/11 oz frozen whole-leaf spinach
400 g/14 oz strong plain flour
2 eggs
1 egg yolk

Cook the spinach in boiling salted water and drain well, squeezing out as much water as possible until the spinach looks quite dry. Finely chop it until it has almost become a 'paste'.

Heap the flour on to a flat working surface and make a deep well in the centre. Break the eggs into the well, add the yolk and, using a fork, lightly beat the eggs. Add the chopped spinach a little at a time while beating the flour into the eggs.

Continue as for fettuccine.

Cook's Tip

Green pasta is slightly moister than plain pasta so remember to flour the working surface well before rolling out the dough. Red-coloured pasta can be obtained by adding concentrated tomato purée instead of the spinach. Yellow pasta can be made by adding saffron.

POTATO GNOCCHI

(GNOCCHI DI PATATE)

Illustrated opposite
400 g / 14 oz old potatoes
about 200 g / 7 oz plain flour
1 teaspoon salt
1 egg

Scrub the potatoes, but do not peel, and boil them whole for approximately 30–40 minutes, until they are cooked through. Drain and allow them to cool.

Sieve three-quarters of the flour with the salt on to a flat working surface, making a well in the centre. When the potatoes are tepid, peel and mash them making sure that there are no lumps. Put the mashed potatoes in the well in the middle of the flour, add the egg and, moving from the inside outwards, work the flour into the potato and egg to make a smooth paste which resembles a soft pastry dough, using part of the remaining flour if necessary.

Cut the dough into smaller sections and roll them out into thin sausage-shaped rolls the thickness of a finger. Using a sharp knife, cut the rolls into lengths of between $1-1.5$ cm/$\frac{1}{2}-\frac{3}{4}$ in. The pieces will resemble small cushions. Shape the gnocchi by pressing your index finger into the centre of each one to make a dent, or by rolling them down the prongs of a fork, using your thumb. The pressure of your thumb against the fork will make the gnocchi slightly concave, and the fork will make the gnocchi ridged.

Sprinkle the prepared gnocchi with a little flour and place them on a lightly floured surface to prevent them from sticking together.

Drop the gnocchi in two or three batches into plenty of boiling salted water. The gnocchi will rise to the surface when they are ready and when the water reaches boiling point again (3–4 minutes), lift the gnocchi out of the water using a draining spoon. Drain the gnocchi well in a colander and put them into a serving dish with a ladle of hot sauce. Stir well and keep the serving dish hot by placing it over the pan of sauce until the gnocchi are all ready. With each batch of gnocchi add a ladle of sauce and a little grated Parmesan.

Serve individual portions with more grated Parmesan.

Sauce choice Ragoût (page 57), in the winter, Tomato and Fresh Basil (page 37), in the summer

COOK'S TIP

Potato gnocchi are best made, cooked and served immediately. The potatoes must be cooked in their skins to prevent them from absorbing any water. The quantity of flour used will vary depending on the quality of the potatoes. A more watery potato will take up more flour and a floury potato less. New potatoes cannot be used for making gnocchi as they contain too much water. The gnocchi are often served in the 'cushion' shape, but if you manage to master the art of rolling them down a fork, they will cook through better and hold more sauce in their hollow shape.

Potato Gnocchi
Shaping Gnocchi

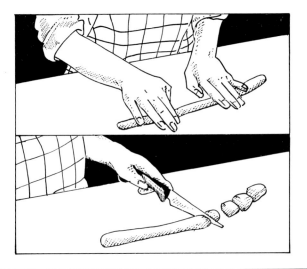

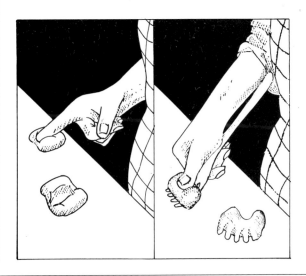

RAVIOLI WITH RICOTTA CHEESE AND SPINACH

(RAVIOLI CON RICOTTA E SPINACI)

Illustrated on page 78

STUFFING
200 g/7 oz frozen whole-leaf spinach
250 g/9 oz ricotta cheese
1 egg plus 1 egg yolk
25 g/1 oz Parmesan cheese, grated
$\frac{1}{4}$ teaspoon grated nutmeg
salt and freshly ground black pepper

PASTA
4 eggs
400 g/14 oz strong plain flour
plus flour for working

SHAPING
$\frac{1}{2}$ beaten egg

Cook the spinach in boiling salted water, drain well and squeeze out as much water as possible. Finely chop, mince or pass the spinach through a sieve. Mix the spinach with the ricotta cheese, egg, egg yolk, grated cheese and nutmeg, seasoning to taste. Leave to stand in the refrigerator for 2–3 hours.

Heap the flour on to a flat work surface and make a deep well in the centre. Break the eggs into the well. Using a fork, lightly beat the eggs and gradually start incorporating the flour, taking it from the bottom inside of the well.

Continue incorporating the flour into the eggs with the fork, taking care not to break the sides of the well or the eggs will escape, until you have a thickish mixture. Continue with your hands, working from the inside outwards until you have a soft dough and all the flour has been incorporated. While working the flour into the egg keep scraping the work surface and rubbing your hands with flour so that all the mixture that has stuck to your hands or the table can be rubbed off and incorporated into the dough.

Knead the dough for about 10 minutes, using the heel of your palms and a rhythmic peddling movement to work the dough into a roll, fold in the ends and start again. The finished dough should be smooth and fairly firm to the touch.

Leave the dough to rest for 5–6 minutes, covering it with a bowl to prevent the surface from drying out.

Knead the dough once more into a roll and twist it into two equal pieces. Using a long rolling pin, roll out the dough into two circles of equal size. While rolling out the second piece, keep the first one folded over to help retain its moisture. When the second circle is the same size as the first, sprinkle it with flour and roll it around the rolling pin. Lay the first circle flat on the working surface and brush it with a little beaten egg and water.

Cover the pasta with rows of little piles of stuffing (1 generous teaspoon each), placing them about 2.5 cm/1 in apart from one another. Gently unroll the second sheet of pasta off the rolling pin on to the top of the first. Press the two sheets of pasta together around the piles of stuffing and cut them, using a pastry wheel, into ravioli about 2.5 cm/1 in square. Sprinkle the prepared ravioli with flour and place them on a well floured surface to prevent them from sticking together.

Drop the ravioli into a large open pan of fast boiling salted water, and lift them out with a draining spoon approximately 5 minutes after the water has come back to a fast boil.

Serve immediately with your favourite sauce.

Sauce choice Butter (page 72), Tomato and Fresh Basil (page 37), Bolognese (page 56).

COOK'S TIP
Best made, cooked and eaten the same day. Ravioli will, however, keep in the refrigerator until the next day.

Note: 'ravioli' in Rome are always square and 'agnolotti' are always round or half-moon shaped. The shape, however, varies according to which recipe book you read or the part of Italy you are in. Some people maintain that ravioli are round.

TORTELLINI ALLA GRAND HOTEL

PASTRY CASES
300 g/11 oz rough puff or flaky pastry
a little beaten egg to glaze

FILLING
200 g/7 oz mushrooms
1 clove garlic
25 g/1 oz butter
salt
200 ml/7 fl oz single cream
25 g/1 oz Parmesan cheese, grated
400 g/14 oz tortellini (illustrated recipe
pages 90–92)
2 chicken stock cubes
1 tablespoon chopped parsley to garnish

Roll out the pastry to a thickness of about 3 mm/ $\frac{1}{8}$ in and cut eight circles about 10 cm/4 in. in diameter. Cut out the centres from four of the circles, leaving a border of about 1.5 cm/$\frac{3}{4}$ in. Damp the rings and press them on to the circles, pricking them lightly so that they will rise evenly.

Place the circles on a greased baking tray together with the centres of the cut circles and put them in the refrigerator for about 30 minutes.

Glaze the pastry with a little beaten egg and bake in a moderately hot oven (200 C, 400 F, gas 6) for about 20 minutes, until well risen and golden brown. Keep warm in the oven.

Clean the mushrooms and chop them into small pieces. Peel the garlic and cut it in half. Melt the butter in a large frying pan and gently fry the garlic until it is golden. Add the chopped mushrooms and fry until tender. Salt to taste and remove the garlic. Stir the cream into the mushrooms in the pan, adding the grated Parmesan and a little boiling pasta water.

While cooking the mushrooms, cook the tortellini in boiling water, to which the two chicken stock cubes have been added as well as a little salt. Drain them well when cooked and mix them with the cream and mushroom sauce.

Pile the tortellini into the vol-au-vent cases. Put the 'lids' on the cases and garnish each one with a little parsley.

Pasta choice tortellini or mini ravioli stuffed with meat.

SEMOLINA GNOCCHI

(GNOCCHI DI SEMOLA)

1 litre/1$\frac{3}{4}$ pints fresh milk
250 g/9 oz semolina
50 g/2 oz butter
3 eggs
100 g/4 oz Parmesan cheese, grated
$\frac{1}{2}$ teaspoon grated nutmeg
salt

Bring the milk to the boil and slowly sprinkle in the semolina, stirring all the time. Add 20 g/$\frac{3}{4}$ oz of butter and stir the semolina over a low heat for approximately 15 minutes until it is cooked, making sure there are no lumps. Take the pan off the heat and beat in the eggs one by one, followed by the remaining butter and the grated cheese. Add the grated nutmeg and salt to taste.

Pour the mixture out on to a flat, slightly damp working surface. With a slightly dampened hand, flatten the mixture down until it is approximately 1 cm/$\frac{1}{2}$ in thick.

Leave the mixture to cool. When it is cold, cut it into circles of about 5 cm/2 in. in diameter, using a pastry cutter with a fluted edge.

Arrange the gnocchi, slightly overlapping each other, in rows in a greased ovenproof dish. Sprinkle them with more grated Parmesan and flakes of butter.

Bake at the top of a moderately hot oven (200 C, 400 F, gas 6) for about 20 minutes until the gnocchi are golden brown.

Note: the traditional shape for these gnocchi is a circle, but you can cut any shape you wish: hearts or diamonds for example.

MAKING FRIENDS WITH PASTA

NOTES ON THE RECIPES FOR SAUCES

'Why don't you come round for a "spaghettata"?' is a common invitation in Italy. A 'spaghettata' means sitting down to a dish of pasta and a glass of wine, perhaps followed by fresh fruit. The classical 'spaghettata' is spaghetti served with some type of quickly-made sauce, such as tomato or oil and garlic.

Friends get together for an evening to chat, listen to music or play cards and finish by having a 'spaghettata', even though it may be the early hours of the morning. An evening at the cinema or theatre is often followed by a quick visit to a trattoria for a dish of pasta. The occasions for having a 'spaghettata' are never ending. A popular Italian custom, especially in the south, at the end of a really rich and elaborate meal often lasting several hours such as a wedding reception, is to end the meal by calling for a plate of spaghetti with oil and garlic. The Italians say that it helps one to digest!

Pasta is one of the most versatile foodstuffs, which can be kept in the store cupboard and used at a moment's notice, when you haven't had time to do the shopping, for example, or when unexpected visitors turn up on your doorstep. Pasta can make entertaining a pleasure instead of a problem! A nutritious meal can be prepared in minutes and the housewife can enjoy a day out with the family instead of having to stay at home to watch the roast in the oven.

1 All the quantities given serve four people.
2 An indication of the quantity of olive oil has not always been given as an experienced pasta cook never measures the oil, but gets used to his/ her own saucepan sizes and simply 'coats' the bottom of the pan with oil. However, for beginners, the quantity is about 3 tablespoons of oil for a pan 20 cm/8 in. in diameter.
3 Some sauces improve in flavour if made the day before, some must be freshly made before cooking the pasta and others must be made while the pasta is cooking. Each recipe indicates which method is best.
4 All sauces made with cream will be very quickly absorbed by the pasta and should therefore be served and eaten as quickly as possible to avoid the pasta becoming too dry.
5 If you are using a sauce without tomatoes, when draining the freshly cooked pasta it is a good idea to put a small pan or bowl under the colander in case a little pasta water is needed when mixing the pasta with the sauce.
6 The usual serving of pasta is between 100– 150 g/4–5 oz per person, depending on whether you are serving it as a first or main course and how large your appetite is.
7 There are never ending 'variations on a theme', and once you have mastered the art of cooking pasta successfully you can experiment with sauce-making, adding or subtracting various ingredients, inventing new recipes and serving pasta with your favourite flavours, whatever they may be!

Spaghetti with Tomato and Fresh Basil Sauce (page 37)

TOMATO AND VEGETABLE SAUCES

BASIC TOMATO SAUCE

(AL POMODORO)

575 g/1¼ lb canned tomatoes
1 medium onion
olive oil
salt
50 g/2 oz Parmesan cheese, grated

Make the sauce before cooking the pasta. Crush the tomatoes or blend them briefly in a liquidiser. Finely chop the onion. Coat the base of a large frying pan with olive oil. When the oil is hot, but not smoking, add the chopped onion and fry gently until it becomes transparent.

Add the tomatoes and simmer for about 20 minutes, adding salt to taste and stirring occasionally to prevent sticking. The sauce when cooked should be denser and darker in colour.

When cooked, transfer the pasta to a serving dish, and pour the sauce over the top.

Serve individual portions with grated Parmesan.

Pasta choice spaghetti, linguine, conchiglie, penne

COOK'S TIP
If fresh tomatoes are used, they should be peeled and cooked for about 10 minutes only to conserve their fresh flavour.

TOMATO SAUCE WITH OIL AND GARLIC

(AGLIO, OLIO, POMODORO)

4 cloves garlic
575 g/1¼ lb canned tomatoes
olive oil
salt

Start preparing the sauce just before cooking the pasta.

Peel the garlic cloves and cut each one into three or four pieces. Crush the tomatoes or blend them briefly in a liquidiser.

Thickly coat the base of a large frying pan with olive oil. When the oil is hot, but not smoking, add the garlic and fry gently until golden. Add the tomatoes and salt to taste and simmer gently for approximately 10 minutes, until the sauce becomes denser and is cooked.

When the pasta is cooked, transfer it to a serving dish and pour the sauce over the top.

Parmesan cheese is not usually used, but can be served if desired.

Pasta choice spaghetti, penne, conchiglie, farfalle

COOK'S TIP
Should the garlic burn the sauce will have a bitter taste, so throw it away and start again!

Note: this is one of the sauces served most frequently in Italian families, and a favourite for the famous 'spaghettata'.

RAW TOMATO AND FRESH BASIL SAUCE

(POMODORO E BASILICO-CRUDO)

450 g/1 lb ripe tomatoes
3 tablespoons olive oil
1 clove garlic, crushed
bunch of fresh basil
salt

Prepare the sauce before cooking the pasta.

Peel the tomatoes and blend them briefly in a liquidiser. Add the oil and crushed garlic. Wash and dry the basil leaves, discarding the stalks. Add the basil leaves to the sauce, tearing them into small pieces between your fingers.

Leave the sauce to stand for approximately 30 minutes. Add salt to taste and stir well.

When the pasta is cooked, transfer it to a serving dish and pour the sauce over the top.

Serve immediately.

Pasta choice tubetti, penne, conchiglie, farfalle

COOK'S TIP

This is a summer sauce. The raw tomatoes served with the hot pasta make a pleasant combination. The salt must be added at the last minute to avoid the tomatoes becoming soft and watery.

TOMATO AND FRESH BASIL SAUCE

(POMODORO E BASILICO)

Illustrated on page 35

675 g/1½ lb ripe tomatoes
1 clove garlic
bunch of fresh basil
olive oil
salt
50 g/2 oz Parmesan cheese, grated
(optional)

Make the sauce before cooking the pasta.

Peel and crush the tomatoes or blend them briefly in a liquidiser. Peel the garlic clove and cut it into three or four pieces. Pick the basil leaves off the stalks, wash and dry them. Discard the stalks.

Coat the base of a large frying pan with olive oil. When the oil is hot, but not smoking, add the garlic and fry until golden. Add the tomatoes and half the basil leaves, tearing them into pieces with your fingers. Salt to taste.

Cook for approximately 10 minutes, until the sauce becomes denser and darker in colour. Turn off the heat and add the rest of the basil, tearing it between your fingers.

When the pasta is cooked, transfer it to a serving dish and pour the sauce over the top.

Serve individual portions with grated Parmesan, if liked.

Pasta choice spaghetti, penne, rigatoni

COOK'S TIP

To peel the tomatoes, make a small cut in the skins, put the tomatoes in a bowl and cover them with boiling water. Leave for a few minutes, after which the skins will be easy to remove.

OIL AND GARLIC SAUCE WITH PINE KERNELS AND SULTANAS

(Aglio, Olio, Pinoli e Uva Passa)

Illustrated opposite

bunch of parsley
4 cloves garlic
200 ml/7 fl oz olive oil
1½ generous tablespoons pine kernels, or roughly chopped almonds
1 generous tablespoon sultanas

Start making the sauce when you have dropped the pasta into the boiling salted water.

Wash, dry and roughly chop the parsley. Peel and cut each clove of garlic into three or four pieces.

Put the oil into a small saucepan and when it is hot, but not smoking, add the garlic and 'boil' until golden and crispy. Add the nuts, followed by the sultanas two minutes later. At this point add half the chopped parsley and a ladle of boiling pasta water, just before draining the pasta.

Divide the freshly cooked pasta between four individual dishes, and pour the sauce over each one, taking care to divide the nuts and sultanas as evenly as possible.

Serve immediately, garnished with the remaining chopped parsley.

Pasta choice spaghetti

COOK'S TIP
The secret of this sauce is to get the timing right. It should be ready at the same time as the pasta. It takes quite a bit of practice to do it perfectly. Good luck!

Top: *Spaghetti with Oil and Garlic, Pine Kernel and Sultana Sauce*
Bottom: *Trenette with Genoese Paste (page 42)*

'HOT-TEMPERED' SAUCE

(ALL'ARRABBIATA)

**575 g/1¼ lb canned tomatoes
1 clove garlic
olive oil
1 medium green chilli
salt
1 tablespoon chopped parsley**

Prepare the sauce before cooking the pasta.

Crush the tomatoes or blend them briefly in a liquidiser. Peel and cut the garlic clove into three or four pieces. Slit the chilli, discard the seeds, then rinse and dry the chilli.

Coat the bottom of a large frying pan with the oil. When it is hot, but not smoking, add the garlic and chilli, crushing the chilli against the bottom of the pan to release its flavour. When the garlic is golden, add the tomatoes and cook for about 15 minutes, adding salt to taste.

When the pasta is cooked, transfer it to a serving dish and pour the sauce over the top.

Serve individual portions garnished with the chopped parsley.

Pasta choice penne

COOK'S TIP

This sauce is recommended for hot-curry lovers. Be sure to wash your hands after handling chillies and keep your hands away from your eyes for an hour afterwards. The seeds inside are really hot and the chilli juice can irritate skin and burn eyes. Rinse chillies in cold water, not hot, to avoid the fumes rising to your face.

SAILOR'S SAUCE

(ALLA MARINARA)

**2 (400-g/14-oz) cans tomatoes
2 cloves garlic
small bunch of parsley
olive oil
salt and freshly ground black pepper**

Start making the sauce when you drop the pasta into the boiling salted water.

Crush the tomatoes or blend them briefly in a liquidiser. Peel and cut each clove of garlic into three or four pieces. Wash, dry and roughly chop the parsley.

Coat the bottom of a large frying pan with olive oil and when the oil is hot, but not smoking, add the garlic and fry gently until golden. Add the tomatoes and season to taste. Simmer gently until the pasta is ready.

Transfer the freshly cooked pasta to a serving dish and pour the sauce over the top.

Serve individual portions garnished with chopped parsley.

Pasta choice spaghetti, linguine

COOK'S TIP

This sauce can also be made with fresh, ripe tomatoes which have been peeled, deseeded and finely chopped.

Note: the name 'Sailor's sauce' is due to the fact that the sauce smells of the sea even though no fish has been added.

'LOOSE-LADY' STYLE SAUCE

(ALLA PUTTANESCA)

2 (400-g/14-oz) cans tomatoes
2 cloves garlic
10 black olives
1 tablespoon capers
2 anchovy fillets
olive oil
1 small chilli
2 teaspoons concentrated tomato purée
salt
1 tablespoon chopped parsley

Prepare the sauce before cooking the pasta.

Crush the tomatoes or blend them briefly in a liquidiser. Peel and cut each clove of garlic into three or four pieces. Stone and cut the olives into quarters. Rinse the capers if they have been salted. Finely chop the anchovy fillets and crush them into a paste.

Coat the bottom of an earthenware casserole or frying pan with olive oil. When the oil is hot, but not smoking, add the garlic and the chilli, crushing the chilli against the bottom of the pan to release its flavour. Gently fry the garlic until golden, add the crushed anchovy fillets, olives and capers, stirring all the time. After 2–3 minutes add the tomato purée, the tomatoes and salt to taste. (Remember that the anchovies and capers are already quite salty.) Slowly simmer the sauce for about 30 minutes, stirring occasionally, until the sauce becomes denser and darker in colour.

When the pasta is cooked, transfer it to a serving dish and pour the sauce over the top.

Serve garnished with chopped parsley.

Pasta choice spaghetti, linguine

COOK'S TIP
The chilli may be omitted and individual portions served with chilli oil. (See recipe on page 48).

Note: this sauce takes its unusual name from those wives who wish to appear as though they have been slaving over a hot stove all day preparing a special sauce for their husbands instead of devoting their time to other gentlemen! It was also, apparently, the sauce made most often in the brothels, between one client and the next!

SAUCE LUCIO'S STYLE

(ALLA LUCIO)

2 cloves garlic
450 g/1 lb ripe tomatoes
small bunch of fresh basil
olive oil
1 chilli
salt
50 g/2 oz Parmesan cheese, grated

Start preparing the sauce just before cooking the pasta.

Peel and cut each garlic clove into three or four pieces. Cut each tomato into eight pieces, discarding the cores. Wash and dry the basil leaves, discarding the stalks.

Coat the bottom of a large frying pan with olive oil and when the oil is hot, but not smoking, add the garlic and chilli and fry gently until the garlic is golden, crushing the chilli against the bottom of the pan to release its flavour. Add the tomatoes and cook until soft over a strong heat so that they rapidly lose their liquid and do not boil but fry. Salt to taste. Add the fresh basil, breaking it into small pieces between your fingers.

When the pasta is cooked and drained, put it back into the hot pan where it was cooked, add the sauce and the Parmesan and mix thoroughly. The heat of the pasta, the sauce and the saucepan will melt the cheese and it will mix with the tomatoes, making a creamy sauce which coats the pasta.

Serve immediately.

Pasta choice penne, pennette, rigatoni, sedani

COOK'S TIP
Should the tomato skins in the sauce bother you, peel the tomatoes before using them.

GENOESE PASTE

(PESTO GENOVESE)

Illustrated on pages 38 and 39

**2 large bunches of fresh basil
4 leaves of fresh mint
1 clove garlic
1 tablespoon pine kernels, or chopped
almonds, or chopped walnuts
50 g/2 oz pecorino cheese, grated
about 150 ml/¼ pint olive oil**

Start making the sauce just before cooking the pasta.

Wash and dry the basil and mint leaves. Peel the garlic clove and chop it into small pieces. Put the basil, mint and garlic on to a large chopping board and finely chop them together until a very thick paste is formed, adding the nuts and part of the grated cheese as you chop.

Scrape the mixture into a bowl, add the rest of the grated cheese and gradually beat in the olive oil.

Just before draining the pasta, take a ladle of boiling pasta water and mix it with the paste in the bowl.

Transfer the freshly cooked pasta to a serving dish, and pour the paste over the top, adding a little more pasta water if necessary. The paste should be thick and creamy and coat the pasta.

Serve individual portions with a little extra pecorino or with Parmesan cheese if desired.

Pasta choice Pesto Genovese is traditionally served with trenette (flat spaghetti), but can also be served with spaghetti or fettuccine.

COOK'S TIP

The basil, mint, garlic and nuts can be put in a food processor and the cheese and oil added afterwards. This makes the preparation very quick and the results are still excellent. Parmesan can be substituted for pecorino if preferred.

ASPARAGUS SAUCE

(CON ASPARAGI)

Illustrated opposite

**900 g/2 lb asparagus
salt
100 g/4 oz butter
100 g/4 oz Parmesan cheese, grated**

Make the sauce before cooking the pasta.

Clean the asparagus and boil them in salted water until cooked, but not too soft. Discard the stalks, leaving only the green and purple spears. Cut these into 2.5-cm/1-in lengths.

Melt the butter in a large frying pan and sauté the asparagus for a few minutes.

When the pasta is cooked, transfer it to a serving dish and add the asparagus with the grated Parmesan. Mix well, adding a little pasta water if necessary to keep the mixture moist.

Serve immediately with a little more grated Parmesan if desired.

Pasta choice penne, sedani, rigatoni

COOK'S TIP

If fresh asparagus is not available then frozen can be used in the same way. Should you use tinned asparagus, just sauté it in the butter. Cream can be added to this sauce if liked.

Penne with Asparagus Sauce

'GAY' SAUCE

(ALLA CHECCA)

400 g/14 oz ripe tomatoes
10 green olives
small bunch of fresh basil
small bunch of parsley
6 tablespoons olive oil
pinch of fennel seeds
salt and freshly ground black pepper

Prepare the sauce before cooking the pasta.

Peel, deseed and roughly chop the tomatoes. Stone the olives and cut each one into two or three pieces. Finely chop the basil leaves and parsley, discarding the stalks.

Pour the olive oil into a serving dish and add the chopped tomatoes, basil, parsley, olives and fennel seeds. Season with salt and black pepper.

When the pasta is cooked, add it to the sauce and mix well.

Serve immediately.

Pasta choice spaghetti, linguine

COOK'S TIP

Olives are best bought in a delicatessen. Try using a cherry stoner to stone the olives, but if you don't possess this handy gadget, halve the olives, using a small serrated knife, and remove the stones.

Note: fennel in Italian is '*finocchio*', which is also the name given to homosexuals in Roman dialect!

CAULIFLOWER SAUCE

(CON CAVOLFIORE)

Illustrated on pages 50 and 51

1 medium cauliflower
salt
10 black olives
1 tablespoon capers
2 cloves garlic
olive oil

Prepare the sauce before cooking the pasta.

Break the cauliflower into florets and boil in salted water until almost cooked. Strain, reserving a glass of cauliflower water. Stone and cut each olive into three or four pieces. Rinse and dry the capers if they have been salted. Peel and cut the cloves of garlic into three or four pieces each.

Coat the bottom of a large saucepan with olive oil and gently fry the garlic until golden. Add the capers and olives and fry gently for approximately 5 minutes, until they have begun to soften. Add the strained cauliflower and stir well, adding the glass of cauliflower water to keep the mixture moist.

Drain the pasta 2–3 minutes before it is completely cooked and add it to the cauliflower sauce in the saucepan. Cook the pasta for the last few minutes in the cauliflower sauce, adding a little pasta water if necessary to keep the mixture moist.

Serve as it is. Cheese is not usually used.

Pasta choice conchiglie, tubetti, pasta mista

COOK'S TIP

Some people prefer to cook the pasta in the cauliflower water once the cauliflower has been removed.

BROCCOLI SAUCE

(CON BROCCOLI)

450 g/1 lb broccoli, trimmed and washed
salt and freshly ground black pepper
50 g/2 oz butter
100 g/4 oz Parmesan cheese, grated

Cook the broccoli in boiling salted water until just tender. Drain, reserving the water, then cook the pasta in the broccoli water. Some people manage to cook the two together but you must get the timing right so that both are cooked to perfection. Keep the broccoli warm until the pasta is ready.

Transfer the freshly cooked pasta to a serving dish. Cut the broccoli into small pieces and mix it with the pasta, adding the butter and half the grated Parmesan. Mix well, adding plenty of freshly ground black pepper and a little pasta water if necessary to keep the mixture moist.

Serve with the remaining Parmesan.

Pasta choice orecchiette, conchiglie, pipe

COOK'S TIP
Some people prefer to add crispy bacon cubes and their fat instead of butter. Remove the rind from streaky bacon, then cut the rashers into squares. Heat the bacon slowly in a heavy-based frying pan until the fat runs, then continue to cook until crisp. Add to the pasta as above. In this case it is better to use pecorino cheese instead of Parmesan. Chilli can be added, too.

ARTICHOKE SAUCE

(AI CARCIOFI)

Illustrated on pages 46 and 47

4 medium globe artichokes
juice of $\frac{1}{2}$ lemon
25 g/1 oz rindless lean streaky bacon
1 small onion
50 g/2 oz butter
1 tablespoon olive oil
$\frac{1}{2}$ glass dry white wine
$\frac{1}{2}$ stock cube dissolved in 150 ml/$\frac{1}{4}$ pint of water
salt and pepper
50 g/2 oz Parmesan cheese, grated

Prepare the artichokes by pulling off the tough outside leaves until the whitish underneath leaves are exposed. Cut off the top of the artichokes to eliminate the tips of the leaves. Peel the stalks, leaving the tender cores. Rub the prepared artichokes with lemon juice and leave them in cold water and lemon juice for 15 minutes.

Finely chop the bacon and onion and gently fry them in half the butter and the olive oil, until the onion becomes transparent and the bacon crispy. Drain the artichokes well and cut them lengthways into thin wedges and the stalks into thin strips. Add them to the bacon and onion and, stirring all the time, slowly add the white wine, letting it evaporate. Add the dissolved stock cube and simmer gently for approximately 20 minutes, until the artichokes are tender and the sauce has become denser. Season to taste.

When the pasta is cooked, reserve some of the pasta water before transferring the pasta to a serving dish. Pour the sauce over the top, adding the remaining butter and the Parmesan to form a moist, creamy mixture. Should it appear too dry, add a little of the reserved pasta water.

Serve individual portions with extra Parmesan if desired.

Pasta choice orecchiette, fettuccine, linguine

COOK'S TIP
Cream can be added to the sauce if desired, but this makes an extremely rich and filling dish. The artichokes are rubbed with lemon juice to prevent them from becoming discoloured and to take away their bitter taste.

PREPARING ARTICHOKES

1   Remove the stalks and peel them, leaving the tender cores.

2   Cut off the base and pull off the tough outside leaves until the whitish underneath leaves are exposed.

3   Cut off the tops of the artichokes to eliminate the tips of the leaves.

4   Remove and discard the inner core of leaves and take out the bitter choke.

5   Rub the prepared artichokes with lemon juice and leave them in cold water and lemon juice for 15 minutes. This removes their bitter taste and prevents the artichokes from turning brown.

6   Drain the artichokes well and cut them lengthways into thin wedges and the stalks into thin strips.

Orecchiette with Artichoke Sauce (page 45)

OIL AND GARLIC SAUCE

(AGLIO, OLIO)

**about 200 ml/7 fl oz olive oil
4 cloves garlic, peeled and chopped
1 small green chilli
1 tablespoon chopped parsley to garnish**

Start making the sauce a few minutes before the pasta is ready to serve. Heat the olive oil in a small frying pan. Add the garlic and chilli. Fry gently until the garlic is crispy and golden brown, crushing the chilli against the bottom of the pan to release its flavour.

Transfer the freshly cooked pasta to a serving dish and pour the sauce over the top immediately.

Serve garnished with the chopped parsley.

Pasta choice spaghetti

COOK'S TIP
The chilli can be omitted for people who do not like hot dishes and individual portions can be served with chilli oil.

Chilli oil Put four or five crushed chillies in a clean, dry jam jar or small bottle and cover with as much oil as desired. Leave to stand in a cool, dry place for at least a week. The oil will then be ready to use as required. The chilli flavour will vary according to how hot the chillies are and to the quantity of oil used. Try using only a few drops to begin with if you are not sure of the strength.

A quick way to chop parsley Put parsley sprigs in a mug and snip them with scissors. This method does not produce as fine a result as using a knife and board, but it is more practical for small amounts of parsley.

SWEETCORN SAUCE

(AL MAIS)

**1 medium onion
50 g/2 oz butter
200 ml/7 fl oz single cream
1 (340-g/12-oz) can sweetcorn, drained
salt and pepper**

Start making the sauce before cooking the pasta.

Finely mince the onion so that it becomes a pulp. Melt the butter in a large saucepan and gently fry the onion, covering the pan to prevent the onion from becoming brown and adding a little water if necessary. Cook until the onion is soft and creamy. Add the cream and the drained sweetcorn and heat through gently, seasoning.

While the pasta is cooking, add a ladle of boiling pasta water to the sauce and mix thoroughly.

Transfer the freshly cooked pasta to a serving dish and pour the sauce over the top.

Serve immediately, with a little freshly ground black pepper if desired.

Pasta choice mezze maniche, pipe, conchiglie

COOK'S TIP
A tablespoon of grated Parmesan cheese may be added when mixing the pasta with the sauce.

Aubergine Sauce

(Alle Melanzane)

**2 medium aubergines
1 small mozzarella cheese
1 (400-g/14-oz) can tomatoes
1 clove garlic
olive oil
salt
grated Parmesan cheese to serve (optional)**

Make the sauce before cooking the pasta.

Wash, dry and cut the aubergines into 1-cm/½-in cubes. Do not peel them. Cut the mozzarella cheese into small cubes. Crush the tomatoes or blend them briefly in a liquidiser. Peel and cut the garlic clove into three or four pieces.

Coat the bottom of a large frying pan with olive oil. When it is hot, but not smoking, add the garlic and gently fry until golden. Add the aubergines and fry until tender but firm. Salt to taste. Add the tomatoes and cook for a further 10–15 minutes, until the sauce becomes denser.

When the pasta is cooked, transfer it to a serving dish, pour the sauce over the top and mix thoroughly. Add the mozzarella cheese.

Serve individual portions with Parmesan if liked. The mozzarella cheese will melt with the heat of the sauce and the pasta. As you serve the individual portions be careful not to stir the mozzarella into the pasta as it will stick together forming a large lump!

Pasta choice penne, rigatoni, sedani

Cook's Tip
Many types of aubergine impart a bitter flavour to the finished dish. A method of preparing them to avoid this is to salt them beforehand. Wash, dry and cut the aubergines to the required size, then place them in layers, with salt in between, in a colander over a bowl. Leave the aubergine for 30 minutes, then discard the liquid that collects in the bowl and use the aubergine as the recipe directs.

Spinach Sauce

(Con gli Spinaci)

**350 g/12 oz frozen whole-leaf spinach
salt
3 cloves garlic
150 ml/¼ pint olive oil
1 tablespoon pine kernels, or roughly chopped almonds
1 tablespoon sultanas**

Start making the sauce before cooking the pasta.

Cook the spinach in boiling salted water. Drain, squeezing out as much water as possible. Roughly chop the leaves. Peel and cut each garlic clove into three or four pieces.

Heat the oil in a large frying pan and when it is hot, but not smoking, add the garlic and fry until golden. Add the nuts, followed by the sultanas a few minutes later. Add the chopped spinach and sauté for 2–3 minutes.

When the pasta is cooked, transfer it to a serving dish and mix in the sauce.

Serve immediately, as it is.

Pasta choice gnocchetti alla sarda, conchiglie

Cook's Tip
There are many variations of this recipe. Some people prefer to omit the nuts and sultanas, but add chilli. In this case the pasta can be served with grated cheese if desired.

PEPERONI SAUCE

(CON PEPERONI)

Illustrated opposite

**2 medium red peppers
10 black olives
1 tablespoon capers
olive oil
salt
50 g/2 oz butter
100 g/4 oz Parmesan cheese, grated
a little milk**

Prepare the sauce before cooking the pasta.

Wash, dry, deseed and cut the peppers into thin strips lengthways. Stone and cut each olive into three or four pieces. Wash and dry the capers if they have been salted.

Coat the bottom of a large frying pan with olive oil and gently fry the peppers until tender, adding the olives and capers halfway through the cooking time. Salt to taste. Strain off the excess olive oil.

When the pasta is cooked, transfer it to a serving dish and pour the sauce over the top. Add the butter, Parmesan and a drop of milk and mix thoroughly. Add a little more milk if necessary to form a moist, creamy mixture.

Serve individual portions with extra Parmesan if liked.

Pasta choice eliche, fusilli

COOK'S TIP

Eliche and fusilli are used with this sauce so that the long strips of pepper can wrap themselves around the twisted forms of pasta. Peppers cooked in this way are served as a vegetable dish and consequently this pasta is often made with peppers left over from a previous meal.

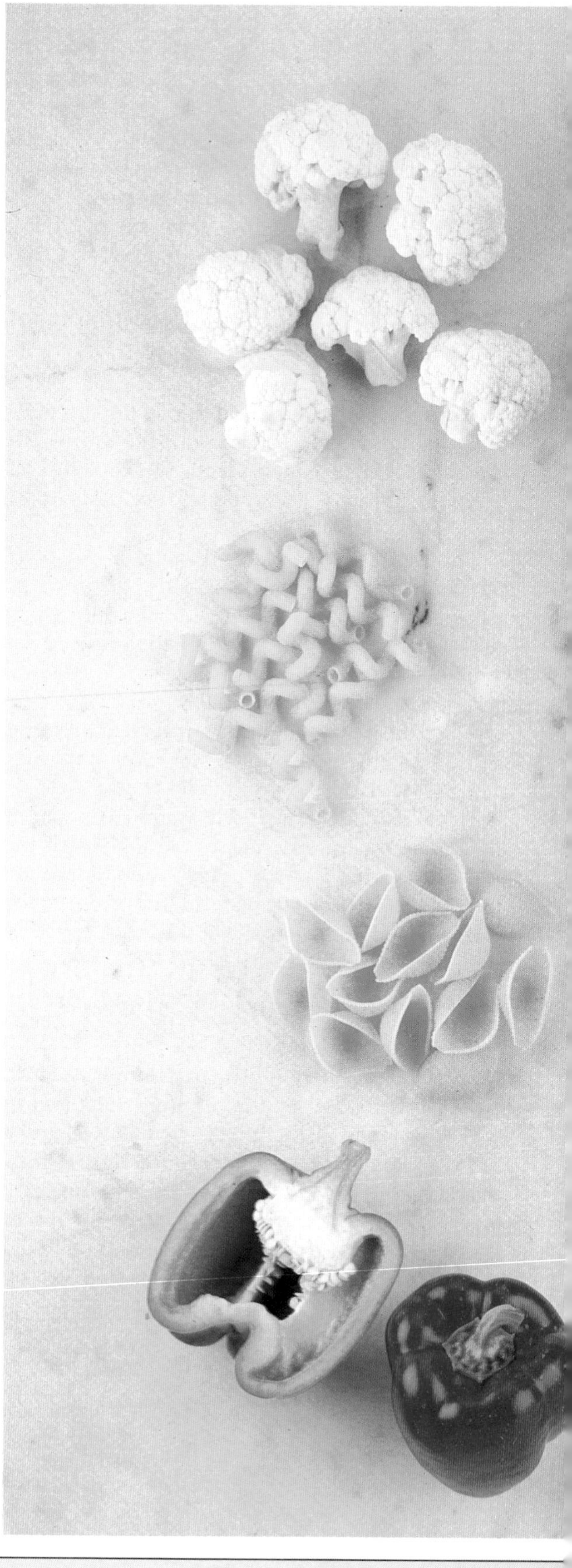

Top: *Conchiglie with Cauliflower Sauce (page 44)*
Bottom: *Fusilli with Peperoni Sauce*

PUMPKIN SAUCE

(CON ZUCCA)

**3 cloves garlic
small bunch of parsley
800 g/1¾ lb pumpkin
olive oil
salt and freshly ground white pepper**

Make the sauce before cooking the pasta.

Peel the garlic and cut each clove into three or four pieces. Wash and roughly chop the parsley. Peel the pumpkin, remove the seeds and cut the flesh into small cubes of about 1.5 cm/¾ in.

Thickly coat the bottom of a large saucepan with olive oil. When the oil is hot, but not smoking, add the garlic and fry gently until golden. Add the pieces of pumpkin, stir well, put the lid on the pan and cook gently, stirring occasionally and adding salt to taste, until the pumpkin is soft. Add the chopped parsley and lots of white pepper.

When the pasta is cooked, transfer it to a serving dish, then mix in the sauce.

Serve as it is or add more pepper if liked.

Pasta choice pasta mista, tubetti, occhi di lupo

COOK'S TIP

Some people prefer to cook the pasta with the pumpkin, but this means that the pumpkin will break down considerably in the cooking and be very mushy. This is one of the few Italian recipes where white pepper is used instead of black.

TRUFFLE SAUCE

(AL TARTUFO)

**75 g/3 oz black truffles
2 anchovy fillets
6 tablespoons olive oil
salt
small bunch of parsley**

Prepare the sauce while the pasta is cooking.

Clean the truffles, carefully take off the outer 'shell' and cut the truffles into very thin slivers, or grate them. Crush the anchovy fillets with a little olive oil and mix thoroughly until you have formed a thick paste. Gradually work in the rest of the oil, adding a pinch of salt if necessary. Wash, dry and roughly chop the parsley.

When the pasta is cooked, transfer it to a serving dish and pour the anchovy oil over the top, add the truffles and mix thoroughly. Sprinkle with chopped parsley.

Serve immediately.

Pasta choice spaghetti, linguine

COOK'S TIP

This is a very old, traditional recipe from Umbria, the region where black truffles are found in season.

CELERY AND OTHER THINGS

(AL SEDANO ED ALTRE COSE)

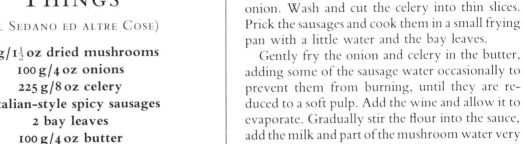

40 g/1½ oz dried mushrooms
100 g/4 oz onions
225 g/8 oz celery
2 Italian-style spicy sausages
2 bay leaves
100 g/4 oz butter
½ glass dry white wine
65 g/2½ oz flour
500 ml/17 fl oz milk
salt
pinch of marjoram
pinch of grated nutmeg
50 g/2 oz Parmesan cheese, grated

Make the sauce before cooking the pasta.

Put the dried mushrooms to soak in about 300 ml/½ pint boiling water. Finely chop the onion. Wash and cut the celery into thin slices. Prick the sausages and cook them in a small frying pan with a little water and the bay leaves.

Gently fry the onion and celery in the butter, adding some of the sausage water occasionally to prevent them from burning, until they are reduced to a soft pulp. Add the wine and allow it to evaporate. Gradually stir the flour into the sauce, add the milk and part of the mushroom water very slowly, stirring all the time. Salt to taste. Cook over a very low heat for approximately 1 hour, stirring frequently and adding a pinch each of marjoram and nutmeg. If the sauce becomes too thick during cooking, add a little more of the mushroom water.

Roughly chop the mushrooms and gently fry them in a knob of butter until tender. Cut the sausages into cubes.

Blend the sauce in a liquidiser until smooth or pass it through a mouli-sieve. When the pasta is cooked, transfer it to a serving dish and pour the sauce over the top, adding the chopped mushrooms and sausages. Mix thoroughly, adding half the grated Parmesan.

Serve individual portions with the remaining grated Parmesan.

Pasta choice penne, conchiglie, lumache, mezze maniche

Note: this was one of the sauces invented to launch *marille* a new type of pasta produced by Voiello of Naples.

COURGETTE SAUCE

(ALLE ZUCCHINE)

Illustrated opposite

8 medium–small courgettes
2 medium onions
olive oil
salt
50 g/2 oz Parmesan cheese, grated

Prepare the sauce before cooking the pasta.

Wash, dry and slice the courgettes into thin circles. Finely chop the onions.

Coat the base of a large frying pan with olive oil and gently fry the onions until transparent. Add the courgettes halfway through the onion cooking time and fry them gently until just tender. Stir frequently to prevent burning and sticking. Put a lid on the pan if the courgettes tend to burn on the outside before being cooked through. Salt to taste.

When draining the pasta, collect a small quantity of the cooking water in a small bowl or pan placed under the colander. Transfer the freshly cooked pasta to a serving dish and mix in the courgettes and onions, adding a ladle of pasta water and the Parmesan to form a moist, creamy mixture.

Serve immediately with a little extra Parmesan if desired.

Pasta choice orecchiette, rigatoni, sedani

COOK'S TIP
Should they be attached the courgette flowers can be washed, sliced and added to the courgettes and onions while frying. These have a very delicate flavour.

SPRINGTIME SAUCE

(SALSA PRIMAVERA)

small bunch of parsley
50 g/2 oz rindless lean streaky bacon
1 medium onion
1 medium carrot
1 stalk celery
100 g/4 oz butter
100 g/4 oz peas
2 ripe tomatoes
1 large courgette
100 g/4 oz mushrooms
1 stock cube
salt and pepper
100 g/4 oz Parmesan cheese, grated

Prepare the sauce before cooking the pasta.

Finely chop the parsley. Cut the bacon into thin strips. Chop together the onion, carrot and celery.

Gently fry the prepared ingredients in half the butter until soft. Add the peas, the tomatoes cut into small pieces, the courgette cut into 1-cm/$\frac{1}{2}$-in cubes and the thinly sliced mushrooms. Add the stock cube dissolved in a ladle of boiling water and simmer gently until all the ingredients are well cooked, seasoning to taste.

When the pasta is cooked, transfer it to a serving dish and add the remaining butter. Add the vegetables and half the grated Parmesan and mix well together.

Serve individual portions with extra grated Parmesan if liked.

Pasta choice penne, rigatoni, conchiglie

COOK'S TIP
Different vegetables may be substituted or added to make many variations on a theme.

Rigatoni with Courgette Sauce

MEAT SAUCES

BOLOGNESE SAUCE

(ALLA BOLOGNESE)

Illustrated on page 58

575 g/1¼ lb canned tomatoes
1 medium onion
1 medium carrot
1 stick celery
1 clove garlic
olive oil
150 g/5 oz lean minced beef
1 glass dry white wine
1 tablespoon concentrated tomato purée
salt
butter and Parmesan cheese to serve

It is best to make the sauce well in advance, even the day before serving.

Crush the tomatoes or blend them briefly in a liquidiser. Finely chop the onion, carrot and celery. Peel and cut the garlic clove in half.

Coat the bottom of an earthenware casserole or saucepan with olive oil. Fry the garlic until golden, add the chopped onion, carrot and celery and continue frying gently until the onion becomes transparent and the carrot and celery become softer.

Stirring all the time, add the minced beef and continue frying until it has browned and is without lumps. Add the wine and when it has evaporated add the tomato purée and tomatoes. Salt to taste and simmer gently for about 45 minutes, adding a little water if the sauce becomes too dense and sticks to the bottom of the pan. When ready the sauce should be dense and dark in colour.

When the pasta is cooked, transfer it to a serving dish and pour the sauce over the top.

Serve individual portions with a knob of butter and grated Parmesan cheese.

Pasta choice penne, rigatoni, fettuccine, spaghetti

COOK'S TIP

Chopped mushrooms may be added together with the other chopped vegetables if desired.

RAGOÛT SAUCE WITH BEEF ROLLS

(AL RAGÙ)

3 (400-g/14-oz) cans tomatoes
1 medium onion
4 cloves garlic
bunch of parsley
8 medium–small slices of beef (for example, thinly sliced rump steak)
8 wooden cocktail sticks
olive oil
1 glass dry white wine
1 tablespoon concentrated tomato purée
salt
Parmesan cheese to serve

Prepare the sauce the day before serving it if you can.

Crush the tomatoes or blend them briefly in a liquidiser. Finely chop the onion. Peel the garlic and cut each clove in half. Wash and dry the parsley, discarding the stalks. Roll up each slice of beef tightly with a piece of garlic and some parsley in the middle. Secure with a cocktail stick.

Coat the base of an earthenware casserole with oil and gently fry the onion until it becomes transparent. Add the beef rolls and brown them on all sides. Pour in the wine and allow almost all of it to evaporate. Then add the tomatoes, the tomato purée and salt to taste.

Simmer the sauce for $1\frac{1}{2}$–2 hours (a pressure cooker reduces the time to 45 minutes), until the meat is tender and the sauce has become denser and darker in colour, stirring frequently and adding water occasionally to prevent sticking.

When the pasta is cooked transfer it to a serving dish and pour three-quarters of the sauce over the top. Keep the remainder of the sauce to serve with the beef rolls.

Serve with grated Parmesan.

Pasta choice rigatoni, tortiglioni, penne, orecchiette, ziti, mafaldine

COOK'S TIP
There are many ways of filling the beef rolls. Instead of garlic and parsley, carrot, celery and cooked ham can be used. The beef rolls are usually served with chipped potatoes as the second course, or at the next meal.

RAGOÛT SAUCE

(AL RAGÙ)

2 (400-g/14-oz) cans tomatoes
3 cloves garlic
1 medium onion
olive oil
350 g/12 oz lean beef
350 g/12 oz lean pork
1 glass dry white wine
1 tablespoon concentrated tomato purée
salt
225 g/8 oz ricotta cheese (optional)
50 g/2 oz Parmesan cheese, grated

The ragoût sauce improves with standing and should be made well in advance. It is best made the day before serving.

Crush the tomatoes or blend them briefly in a liquidiser. Peel the garlic and cut each clove into two or three pieces. Finely chop the onion.

Coat the bottom of an earthenware casserole with olive oil. Gently fry the garlic until golden and the onion until transparent. Add the two pieces of meat and brown them on all sides. Add the wine and allow it to evaporate. Add the tomato purée and the tomatoes. Salt to taste. Reduce the heat and simmer gently for $2\frac{1}{2}$–3 hours – a pressure cooker reduces this time to 45 minutes, giving excellent results – stirring frequently and adding water occasionally to prevent sticking. The sauce should bubble very slowly. When ready the sauce should be dense and dark in colour.

While the pasta is cooking, put the ricotta cheese in a bowl and mix it with a ladle of boiling pasta water to form a cream. Add half a ladle of sauce and stir thoroughly. Transfer the freshly cooked pasta to a serving dish and pour three-quarters of the sauce over the top.

Serve individual portions topped with 2 tablespoons of the ricotta cheese mixture and grated Parmesan.

Pasta choice zite, mafaldine, penne, rigatoni, sedani

COOK'S TIP
The ricotta cheese topping is optional. The sauce is delicious simply served with Parmesan. The meat from the sauce can be served sliced with the rest of the sauce as a second course, or at the next meal.

Fettuccine with Bolognese Sauce (page 56)

Spaghetti with Coalman's Sauce (page 64)

PIZZA-MAKER SAUCE

(ALLA PIZZAIOLA)

2 (400-g/14-oz) cans tomatoes
2 cloves garlic
3 tablespoons olive oil
4 medium slices braising steak
1 generous teaspoon oregano
salt
50 g/2 oz Parmesan cheese, grated

Make the sauce before cooking the pasta.

Crush the tomatoes or blend them briefly in a liquidiser. Peel the garlic and cut each clove into three or four pieces.

Put the oil, tomatoes, meat, garlic and oregano into an earthenware casserole or large frying pan, adding salt to taste. Gently simmer the sauce for approximately 30 minutes, until it becomes denser and darker in colour, stirring occasionally to prevent sticking. Add a little water if the sauce becomes too dense before the meat is cooked.

When the pasta is cooked, transfer it to a serving dish and pour three-quarters of the sauce over the top. Keep the remaining sauce to serve with the slices of meat as the second course.

Serve individual portions with grated Parmesan.

Pasta choice penne, rigatoni, sedani, zite

COOK'S TIP

This sauce, as the name implies, is made from the ingredients used for pizza toppings (apart from the meat!).

GENOESE SAUCE

(ALLA GENOVESE)

1.25 kg/2½ lb onions
1 clove garlic
olive oil
575 g/1¼ lb lean beef
1 glass dry white wine
salt
50 g/2 oz Parmesan cheese, grated

Prepare the sauce before cooking the pasta. It can be made well in advance of serving, if convenient.

Finely chop or grate the onions. Peel the garlic.

Coat the bottom of an earthenware casserole with olive oil. Gently fry the garlic until golden and brown the piece of meat on all sides. Add the wine and allow it to evaporate. Add the onions slowly, stirring all the time and cook until they have become slightly softer and darker but not burnt. Reduce the heat, add a glass of water and simmer the sauce very slowly, stirring occasionally and adding more water when necessary to prevent sticking. Salt to taste. Cook for about 1½–2 hours – a pressure cooker will reduce the cooking time to 45 minutes – turning the meat slowly round until it is cooked through and the onions have become a creamy, brownish sauce.

When the pasta is cooked, transfer it to a serving dish, and pour three-quarters of the sauce over the top.

Serve individual portions with grated Parmesan.

Pasta choice penne, rigatoni, zite, conchiglie, sedani

COOK'S TIP

The meat can be sliced and served with the rest of the sauce as the second course, or at the next meal. It is traditionally served with chipped potatoes.

Note: this sauce is a very old Neapolitan recipe and does not originate from Genoa as its name implies.

POT ROAST SAUCE

(ARROSTO MORTO)

Illustrated on pages 62 and 63

2 large onions
2 large carrots
2 sticks celery
225 g/8 oz mushrooms
1 clove garlic
100 g/4 oz butter or margarine
2 tablespoons olive oil
575 g/1¼ lb lean beef
1 glass dry white wine
salt
50 g/2 oz Parmesan cheese, grated

This sauce improves with standing and is best made the day before serving.

Finely chop or grate the onions, carrots, celery and mushrooms. Peel the garlic.

Melt 50 g/2 oz butter or margarine in an earthenware casserole together with the olive oil. Add the piece of meat and lightly brown it on all sides. Pour in the wine and allow it to evaporate. Add the garlic and the vegetables slowly, stirring all the time to prevent sticking.

When the vegetables have softened, add enough water to bring the sauce halfway up the sides of the meat. Add salt to taste and simmer for about 1½–2 hours (the use of a pressure cooker will reduce the time to 45 minutes), turning the meat occasionally, until the meat is tender and the sauce has become denser and creamy.

When the pasta is cooked, transfer it to a serving dish and pour three-quarters of the sauce over the top, adding the rest of the butter and mixing thoroughly until the butter has melted.

Serve with grated Parmesan.

Pasta choice fettuccine, tagliatelle, rigatoni, conchiglie, penne

COOK'S TIP
The meat can be sliced and served with the rest of the sauce as the second course or at the next meal.

AMATRICE SAUCE

(ALL' AMATRICIANA)

Illustrated on pages 62 and 63

1 medium onion
4 rindless rashers lean streaky bacon
2 (400-g/14-oz) cans tomatoes
olive oil
1 chilli
1 tablespoon concentrated tomato purée
salt
100 g/4 oz pecorino or romano cheese, grated

Prepare the sauce before cooking the pasta.

Finely chop the onion and cut the bacon into small squares of about 1 cm/½ in. Crush the tomatoes or blend them briefly in a liquidiser.

Coat the bottom of a large frying pan with olive oil and add the chilli and onion. Fry the onion gently until transparent and crush the chilli against the bottom of the pan to release its flavour. Add the bacon and fry until crispy, stirring all the time to prevent it from burning. Add the tomato purée and the tomatoes, salt to taste and simmer gently for approximately 30 minutes, until the sauce becomes denser and darker in colour.

Put half the grated cheese in a serving dish, add the freshly cooked pasta and pour the sauce over the pasta while mixing it with the cheese.

Serve individual portions with more grated cheese if desired.

Pasta choice bucatini, spaghetti, penne

COOK'S TIP
Pecorino has a much stronger flavour than Parmesan. If not liked, Parmesan can be substituted.

Note: Amatrice is a small town to the north-east of Rome, near Rieti.

NORCIA SAUCE

(ALLA NORCINA)

**1 medium onion
olive oil
1 chilli
225 g/8 oz spicy Italian sausage meat
(minced pork flavoured with crushed
peppercorns can be substituted)
1 glass dry white wine
200 ml/7 fl oz single cream
salt
knob of butter
100 g/4 oz Parmesan cheese, grated**

Start making the sauce just before cooking the pasta.

Finely chop the onion. Coat the bottom of a frying pan with olive oil. Add the onion and chilli and fry gently until the onion is transparent, crushing the chilli against the bottom of the pan to release its flavour. Add the sausage meat, stirring all the time so that it does not stick together. Pour in the wine and allow it to evaporate. Continue frying gently until the meat is thoroughly cooked. Add the cream and allow it to heat through, but not to boil.

While the pasta is cooking, add a ladle of boiling pasta water to the sauce. Salt to taste.

Transfer the freshly cooked pasta to a serving dish and pour the sauce over the top, adding a knob of butter and half the grated cheese. Mix thoroughly.

Serve with the remaining Parmesan.

Pasta choice conchiglie, mezze maniche, rigatoni, penne, sedani

Note: Norcia is a town in Umbria which is famous for its sausages and ham.

Top: *Bucatini with Amatrice Sauce (page 61)*
Bottom: *Pot Roast Sauce served with sliced meat as a second course (page 61)*

MINI-MEATBALLS SAUCE

(CON POLPETTINE)

50 g/2 oz day-old bread
warm water or milk
150 g/5 oz finely minced lean beef
2 eggs
1 teaspoon finely grated lemon peel
1 tablespoon chopped parsley
50 g/2 oz Parmesan cheese, grated
salt
50 g/2 oz plain flour
4 cloves garlic
575 g/1¼ lb canned tomatoes
olive oil

Prepare the sauce before cooking the pasta.

Soak the bread in warm water or milk until it softens. Squeeze it out well to eliminate the liquid and crumble the soaked bread between your fingers. Put the minced beef into a bowl, add the bread, eggs, lemon peel, parsley, grated cheese and salt to taste and knead the ingredients together well to form a moist mixture. Shape the mixture into meatballs the size of marbles. Roll the meatballs in the flour and fry them gently in olive oil until they become golden brown.

While frying the first batch of meatballs start preparing the tomato sauce. Peel the garlic cloves and cut each one into three or four pieces. Crush the tomatoes or blend them briefly in a liquidiser. Thickly coat the bottom of a frying pan with olive oil. When the oil is hot, but not smoking, add the garlic and fry gently until golden. Add the tomatoes and salt to taste and simmer the sauce gently until it becomes denser, adding the meatballs as they are cooked. Continue cooking the sauce and meatballs for a further 5 minutes.

When the pasta is cooked, transfer it to a serving dish, and pour the sauce and meatballs over the top. Serve the dish as it is. Parmesan cheese is not usually used.

Pasta choice spaghetti

COOK'S TIP

Try adding pine kernels or chopped nuts to the meatballs as a variation. This makes a very filling one course meal.

COALMAN'S SAUCE

(ALLA CARBONARA)

Illustrated on page 59

4 medium eggs
50 g/2 oz pecorino cheese, grated
50 g/2 oz Parmesan cheese, grated
salt and freshly ground black pepper
4 rindless rashers lean streaky bacon
3 tablespoons olive oil

Prepare the sauce while the pasta is cooking.

Lightly beat the eggs with a fork in a bowl, adding half the grated cheese and seasoning to taste. Cut the bacon into small squares of about 1 cm/½ in.

Gently fry the bacon in the olive oil until it becomes crispy. Turn off the heat. While draining the freshly cooked pasta, turn on the heat under the bacon so that the oil is really hot. As soon as the pasta has been thoroughly drained, put it back in the hot pan where it was cooked and, stirring all the time, pour in the beaten egg and then the bacon and olive oil. On contact with the hot pasta the egg will start to cook and the addition of the boiling oil and bacon turns the egg into a thick creamy sauce which coats the spaghetti.

Serve immediately as the egg will continue to cook for some time and will eventually become too thick and turn the spaghetti into a solid mass! Serve with the remaining mixed grated cheese.

Pasta choice spaghetti, rigatoni

COOK'S TIP

This sauce takes quite a lot of practice to make perfectly, so do not be disappointed if it does not come quite right the first time. Should the egg not cook sufficiently on contact with the pasta and oil you can try putting the pan over the heat for a minute, but you must stir constantly or you will either get scrambled egg forming in the bottom of the pan or the spaghetti will turn into a thick, sticky mass which is impossible to serve.

The secret of this dish is to be as rapid as possible once the pasta is cooked and to keep everything hot so that the egg cooks on contact with the pasta.

Parmesan cheese can be substituted for the pecorino if preferred. The Carbonari were also members of a secret society in Italy at the beginning of the 19th century. This dish may have been named after them, and not the coalmen!

SPICY SAUSAGE SAUCE

(ALLA SALSICCIA)

Illustrated on pages 66 and 67

575 g/1¼ lb canned tomatoes
1 medium onion
4 Italian-style spicy sausages
olive oil
1 glass dry white wine
1 tablespoon concentrated tomato purée
salt
50 g/2 oz Parmesan cheese, grated

Prepare the sauce before cooking the pasta of your choice.

Crush the tomatoes or blend them briefly in a liquidiser. Finely chop the onion. Prick the sausages with a fork to prevent them from bursting and to allow the juices to flow into the sauce. Coat the bottom of a saucepan or earthenware casserole with olive oil.

Gently fry the onion until transparent. Add the sausages and lightly brown them on all sides, then add the wine and allow it to evaporate. Add the tomato purée and tomatoes, salt to taste and simmer for about 40 minutes, until the sausages are thoroughly cooked and the sauce has become denser.

Take the sausages out of the sauce and cut them into thinnish slices.

When the pasta is cooked, place it in a serving dish and pour the sauce over the top, adding the sliced sausages and mixing well.

Serve with grated Parmesan.

Pasta choice mezze maniche, rigatoni, sedani, penne, zite

COOK'S TIP
This is a fairly substantial dish which can be served as a one course meal, especially if a couple of extra sausages are added.

WOOD-CUTTER'S SAUCE

(ALLA BOSCAIOLA)

Illustrated on pages 66 and 67

575 g/1¼ lb ripe tomatoes
225 g/8 oz mushrooms
1 medium onion
2 rindless rashers lean streaky bacon
olive oil
salt and freshly ground black pepper
50 g/2 oz Parmesan cheese, grated

Make the sauce before cooking the pasta.

Peel and crush the tomatoes or blend them briefly in a liquidiser. Clean and thinly slice the mushrooms. Finely chop the onion. Cut the bacon into 1-cm/½-in squares. Coat the bottom of a large frying pan with olive oil and gently fry the onion until it becomes soft and transparent. Add the bacon and mushrooms and fry gently, stirring occasionally until cooked. Add the tomatoes and seasoning to taste and simmer gently for about 20 minutes, until the sauce becomes denser and darker in colour.

When the pasta is cooked, transfer it to a serving dish and pour the sauce over the top.

Serve with grated Parmesan.

Pasta choice penne, rigatoni, sedani, tortiglioni

COOK'S TIP
There are many variations of this sauce. Some people use Parma ham or cooked ham instead of bacon. Some mix cubes of mozzarella cheese with the sauce. The main ingredient is, however, the mushrooms.

GRICIAN SAUCE

(ALLA GRICIA)

6 rindless rashers lean streaky bacon
$\frac{1}{2}$ chilli
150 ml/$\frac{1}{4}$ pint olive oil
50 g/2 oz pecorino or romano cheese,
grated

Make the sauce while cooking the pasta.

Cut the bacon into small squares. Fry the bacon with the chilli in the olive oil, crushing the chilli against the bottom of the pan to release its flavour and frying the bacon until it is crisp.

When the pasta is cooked, place it in a serving dish, pour the sauce over the top, add half the grated cheese and mix thoroughly.

Serve individual portions with the remaining grated cheese.

Pasta choice bucatini, spaghetti, penne

Note: Gricia comes from Griciano which is a village near Amatrice, to the north-east of Rome. In fact, this sauce is very similar to Amatriciana sauce but without the tomatoes.

Top: *Rigatoni and Wood-cutter's Sauce, before the addition of the tomatoes (page 65)*
Bottom: *Mezze Maniche and Spicy Sausage Sauce (page 65)*

CHICKEN LIVER SAUCE

(CON FEGATINI DI POLLO)

350 g/12 oz chicken livers
2 medium onions
olive oil
salt
½ glass dry white wine
50 g/2 oz butter or margarine
50 g/2 oz Parmesan cheese, grated

Make the sauce before cooking the pasta.

Prepare the chicken livers by cutting away all the fat and blood vessels. Coarsely chop them. Finely chop the onions.

Coat the bottom of a frying pan with olive oil and gently fry the onions until transparent, adding the chopped chicken livers. Continue cooking over a low heat until cooked through. Salt to taste.

Take half the chicken livers and onions and mince them, then replace them in the pan. Add the wine and allow it to evaporate.

When the pasta is cooked, place it in a serving dish and pour the sauce over the top. Add the butter and mix well until the butter has melted.

Serve with grated Parmesan.

Pasta choice spaghetti, linguine, fettuccine

COOK'S TIP

The chicken livers have to be minced when they are cooked, otherwise they become a soft mass instead of a fine mince.

FINANCIER-STYLE SAUCE

(ALLA FINANZIERA)

225 g/8 oz chicken livers
100 g/4 oz dried boletus mushrooms
1 medium onion
olive oil
salt and pepper
½ tablespoon plain flour
1 glass dry white wine
50 g/2 oz Parmesan cheese, grated

Prepare the sauce before cooking the pasta.

Clean and trim the chicken livers and chop them into small pieces. Soak the dried mushrooms in a cup of hot water and when they are soft, drain them, keeping half of the soaking water, and cut them into small pieces. Finely chop the onion.

Coat the bottom of a frying pan with olive oil and gently fry the onions until transparent. Add the chicken livers and salt and pepper to taste and fry gently until the livers are cooked. Sprinkle them with the flour and, stirring all the time, add the wine and allow it to evaporate. Add the mushrooms and a little of their soaking water and cook for a further 5–6 minutes.

When the pasta is cooked, place it in a serving dish and pour the sauce over the top, adding a little pasta water if the mixture looks too dry.

Serve individual portions with the grated Parmesan.

Pasta choice fettuccine

COOK'S TIP

If dried boletus mushrooms are not available, fresh field mushrooms can be used instead.

RABBIT SAUCE

(AL CONIGLIO)

1 (675-g/1½-lb) skinned rabbit
½ bottle dry white wine
1 (400-g/14-oz) can tomatoes
2 cloves garlic
olive oil
½ chilli
2 teaspoons concentrated tomato purée
salt
50 g/2 oz Parmesan cheese, grated

The sauce is best made in advance and reheated before serving.

Cut off the rabbit's fore legs and hind legs and cut the body into four pieces, discarding the head and interiors, but keeping the liver and kidneys. Put the pieces of rabbit into a bowl and cover with the wine, reserving half a glass for the sauce. Marinate overnight.

Drain the rabbit and finely mince the liver and kidneys. Crush the tomatoes or blend them briefly in a liquidiser. Peel and crush the garlic.

Thickly coat the bottom of an earthenware casserole or frying pan with olive oil, add the garlic and chilli and fry gently, crushing the chilli against the bottom of the pan to release its flavour. Add the pieces of rabbit and brown them lightly on all sides. Add the minced liver and kidneys and cook slowly, sprinkling the meat with the reserved wine and allowing it to evaporate. Add the tomatoes, tomato purée and salt to taste and simmer gently over a very low heat for at least 1 hour, until the sauce becomes denser and darker in colour and the rabbit is tender. A little water may be added when necessary to prevent the sauce from sticking. When ready the sauce is almost brown in colour. Pour three-quarters of the sauce over the freshly cooked pasta in the serving dish.

Serve individual portions with grated Parmesan cheese if desired.

Pasta choice bucatini, spaghetti, linguine

COOK'S TIP
The rabbit portions can be served as the second course or at the next meal with chipped potatoes.

Note: this is the traditional recipe for cooking rabbit from Ischia. Ischia, although the largest of the islands in the Bay of Naples, is better known for its hunting than its fishing.

CASSEROLE SAUCE

(ALLA CASSERUOLA)

Illustrated on pages 70 and 71

225 g/8 oz button mushrooms
100 g/4 oz butter
225 g/8 oz finely minced lean beef
salt and freshly ground black pepper
½ glass dry white wine
100 g/4 oz Parmesan cheese, grated
knob of butter

Start making the sauce before cooking the pasta.

Wipe and cut the mushrooms into quarters. Melt the butter in an earthenware casserole and gently fry the minced beef, stirring well so that it does not stick together. Add the mushrooms and continue cooking until both the beef and mushrooms are cooked. Add salt to taste and a generous quantity of black pepper. Pour in the wine and allow it to evaporate.

Tip in the drained, freshly cooked pasta and mix thoroughly, adding half the grated Parmesan and a knob of butter.

Serve individual portions immediately with the remainder of the grated Parmesan.

Pasta choice spaghetti, fettuccine, linguine

COOK'S TIP
A little pasta water can be added when mixing everything together if the pasta looks too dry.

CALABRIAN SAUCE

(ALLA CALABRESE)

Illustrated opposite

**575 g/1¼ lb canned tomatoes
2 cloves garlic
olive oil
1 chilli
100 g/4 oz Calabrese salami, thickly sliced
salt
65 g/2½ oz pecorino cheese, grated**

Prepare the sauce before cooking the pasta.

Crush the tomatoes or blend them briefly in a liquidiser. Peel and cut each garlic clove into three or four pieces.

Coat the bottom of a saucepan or earthenware casserole with olive oil. Add the garlic and chilli and fry gently until the garlic is golden, crushing the chilli pepper against the bottom of the pan to release its flavour. Add the tomatoes and the slices of salami. Salt to taste. Simmer gently for about 30 minutes, until the sauce becomes denser and darker in colour.

When the pasta is cooked, place it in a serving dish and pour the sauce over the top.

Serve with the grated pecorino.

Pasta choice penne, rigatoni, conchiglie

Note: in Calabria this sauce is served with grated ricotta which has matured and is no longer a fresh curd cheese.

Top: *Spaghetti with Casserole Sauce (page 69)*
Bottom: *Conchiglie with Calabrian Sauce*

CREAM AND CHEESE SAUCES

BUTTER SAUCE

(AL BURRO)

100 g/4 oz slightly salted butter
100 g/4 oz Parmesan cheese, grated

Cook the pasta of your choice.

Cut the butter into small pieces and place at the bottom of a serving dish.

Drain the freshly cooked pasta, collecting some of the water in a small saucepan or bowl placed underneath the colander. Put the pasta and a ladle of pasta water in the serving dish, then add half the Parmesan. Mix thoroughly until the butter, pasta water and cheese have formed a creamy sauce which coats the pasta. If the mixture appears to be too dry, add a little more pasta water.

Serve immediately with the remaining Parmesan.

Pasta choice all stuffed pasta, spaghetti, linguine, ditali, fettuccine

COOK'S TIP

This is an extremely simple but delicious sauce when made well. If, however, the quantity of water is not right then the pasta can be very dry and unappetising. The sauce is particularly good served with stuffed pasta as it does not interfere with the flavour of the filling.

CREAM OF TOMATO SAUCE

(CREMA DI POMODORO)

1 (400-g/14-oz) can tomatoes
1 small onion
olive oil
salt
200 ml/7 fl oz single cream
50 g/2 oz Parmesan cheese, grated

Prepare the sauce before cooking the pasta.

Crush the tomatoes or blend them briefly in a liquidiser. Finely chop the onion.

Coat the base of a frying pan with olive oil and gently fry the onion until transparent. Add the tomatoes and cook for about 20 minutes, adding salt to taste, until the sauce has become denser.

Pass the sauce through a sieve. Put the sieved sauce and cream into a saucepan and heat gently, stirring all the time until they are thoroughly mixed together and heated through.

When the pasta is cooked, place it in a serving dish and pour the sauce over the top.

Serve individual portions with grated Parmesan.

Pasta choice agnolotti or ravioli stuffed with spinach and ricotta, penne, pipe, rigatoni, sedani

COOK'S TIP

Cream of tomato sauce can also be made by adding cream to sieved versions of Tomato and fresh basil (page 37) and Hot-tempered sauce (page 40).

CHEESE AND PEPPER SAUCE

(CACIO E PEPE)

225 g/8 oz ricotta or fresh, unsalted curd cheese
50 g/2 oz pecorino cheese, grated
freshly ground black pepper

Make the sauce while cooking the pasta.

Mix the ricotta in a bowl with a ladle of boiling pasta water until it becomes a creamy, liquid paste.

Transfer the freshly cooked pasta to the serving dish and pour the ricotta over it, mixing thoroughly and adding the grated pecorino and lots of freshly ground black pepper.

Serve immediately with more grated cheese if desired.

Pasta choice conchiglie, pipe, penne, rigatoni

COOK'S TIP

Ricotta cheese can be made at home easily:

1 litre/1¾ pints milk (not skimmed)
1 tablespoon lemon juice or vinegar (or enough to separate the milk)

Bring the milk to the boil. Add the lemon juice or vinegar, stirring all the time. Leave the mixture to cool.

When tepid pour into a muslin bag, pressing the curd into a solid shape and squeezing out the whey. Leave the cheese to set in the bag placed in a colander to allow the whey to drain away.

When cold, turn out the ricotta cheese on to a plate and use as desired.

This quantity of milk makes approximately 200 g/7 oz ricotta cheese. The quantity of lemon juice may vary according to the acidity of the lemon.

FOUR CHEESES SAUCE

(AI QUATTRO FORMAGGI)

100 g/4 oz Emmental cheese
100 g/4 oz Fontina cheese
25 g/1 oz butter
200 ml/7 fl oz single cream
100 g/4 oz Parmesan cheese, grated

Prepare the sauce while cooking the pasta.

Grate the Emmental and Fontina cheeses. Put the butter and cream in a saucepan and heat slowly, without allowing the cream to boil. Add the grated cheeses and, stirring all the time, allow them to melt and fuse with the cream. Add a ladle of boiling pasta water to thin down the sauce slightly.

Transfer the freshly cooked pasta to a serving dish and pour the sauce over the top.

Serve immediately. Extra Parmesan cheese is not usually served.

Pasta choice pennette, sedani, mezze maniche

COOK'S TIP

This is an extremely rich sauce which needs to be eaten immediately or it will 'gel'.

Different types of cheeses can be substituted and, in fact, this sauce provides a good way of using up leftover bits of cheese which are too small for serving on a cheese board. The Italians cheat a little by calling this 'Four Cheeses Sauce', as it includes only three cheeses, plus the cream, which in Italy tends to be classed as a cheese.

SORRENTO SAUCE

(ALLA SORRENTINA)

Illustrated opposite

575 g/1¼ lb canned tomatoes
2 cloves garlic
bunch of fresh basil
275 g/10 oz mozzarella cheese
olive oil
1 small chilli
salt
50 g/2 oz Parmesan cheese, grated

Make the sauce before cooking the pasta.

Crush the tomatoes or blend them briefly in a liquidiser. Peel the garlic and cut each clove into three or four pieces. Wash and coarsely chop the basil leaves, discarding the stalks. Cut the mozzarella cheese into small cubes of about 1 cm/ ½ in.

Coat the bottom of a frying pan with olive oil. Add the garlic and chilli and fry gently until the garlic is golden, crushing the chilli against the bottom of the pan to release its flavour. Add the tomatoes and a third of the chopped basil, salt to taste and simmer gently for approximately 15 minutes, until the sauce becomes denser.

When the pasta is cooked, transfer it to a serving dish and pour the sauce over the top. Mix the sauce with the pasta and the remainder of the chopped basil. Add the mozzarella cubes but do not stir.

Serve individual portions with grated Parmesan.

Pasta choice penne, sedani

COOK'S TIP

The mozzarella will begin to melt on contact with the hot pasta and sauce. Do not stir it into the pasta as it will stick together to form a solid piece of cheese again.

The chilli may be omitted and chilli oil served with individual portions. (See recipe on page 48).

Top: *Sedani with Sorrento Sauce*
Bottom: *Paglia e Fieno with Ciociara-style Sauce*
(page 77)

CLOTTED CREAM AND WALNUT SAUCE

(AL MASCARPONE E NOCI)

100 g/4 oz walnuts
225 g/8 oz clotted cream
50 g/2 oz Parmesan cheese, grated

Prepare the sauce while the pasta is cooking.

Coarsely chop the walnuts. Heat the clotted cream very gently in a saucepan until it has melted and heated through. Do not allow it to boil. Add the walnuts and a ladle of boiling pasta water to thin down the sauce.

When the pasta is cooked, transfer it to a serving dish and pour the sauce over the top. Add half the grated Parmesan and mix thoroughly.

Serve individual portions immediately with the remaining Parmesan.

Pasta choice conchiglie, pipe

COOK'S TIP

The chopped walnuts get trapped inside the pasta shells so that when biting into the pasta the pleasant nutty flavour is combined with it. This is a very rich sauce and therefore a smaller quantity of pasta (75 g/3 oz per person) than usual should be served.

FLAVIA'S SAUCE

(ALLA FLAVIA)

2 large onions
25 g/1 oz butter
salt
3 generous tablespoons clotted cream
50 g/2 oz Parmesan cheese, grated

Start making the sauce before cooking the pasta.

Finely chop the onions. Melt the butter in a frying pan, add the chopped onions and simmer gently, covering the pan and adding a little water and salt to taste, until the onions become very soft and creamy. Add the clotted cream and heat gently without allowing the sauce to boil.

When the pasta is cooked, transfer it to a serving dish and pour the sauce over the top, adding a little pasta water, a knob of butter and the grated Parmesan. Mix well. The sauce should be thick and creamy.

Serve immediately. Extra Parmesan should not be necessary.

Pasta choice tagliatelle, pennette, conchiglie

Note: this sauce was invented by my sister-in-law, woken one night by hunger!

CIOCIARA-STYLE SAUCE

(ALLA CIOCIARA)

Illustrated on pages 74 and 75

**100 g/4 oz frozen peas
225 g/8 oz button mushrooms
50 g/2 oz butter or margarine
salt and pepper
100-g/4-oz piece lean cooked ham
200 ml/7 fl oz single cream
100 g/4 oz Parmesan cheese, grated**

Prepare the sauce before cooking the pasta.

Cook the peas in boiling salted water and drain. Wipe and thinly slice the mushrooms. Gently fry them in a knob of butter until just tender, adding salt to taste. Trim the fat from the cooked ham and cut the ham into matchsticks.

Put the remaining butter into a saucepan with the cream and heat gently without allowing the mixture to boil. Add the mushrooms with their juice, the peas and the cooked ham. Add a ladle of boiling pasta water and a third of the grated cheese.

When the pasta is cooked, transfer it to a serving dish and pour the sauce over the top.

Serve individual portions with grated Parmesan.

Pasta choice tagliatelle, tagliolini, paglia e fieno, fettuccine, tortellini

Note: Ciociara is a region south of Rome. This sauce, however, is often named 'Tagliatelle alla Pietro', or 'Tagliatelle ai Tre Mori', after the restaurant in which it is served.

CREAM OF MUSHROOM SAUCE

(ALLA CREMA DI FUNGHI)

**400 g/14 oz field mushrooms
1 clove garlic
50 g/2 oz butter or margarine
salt and pepper
$\frac{1}{2}$ glass dry white wine
200 ml/7 fl oz single cream
100 g/4 oz Parmesan cheese, grated**

Prepare the sauce before cooking the pasta.

Wash and chop the mushrooms into 1-cm/$\frac{1}{2}$-in pieces. Peel the garlic.

Melt the butter in the frying pan and gently fry the mushrooms with the garlic until they are just tender and have re-absorbed their juice. Salt to taste. Add the wine and allow it to evaporate. Remove the clove of garlic. Add the cream and, stirring all the time, heat through gently without allowing the mixture to boil. Add a ladle of boiling pasta water.

When the pasta is cooked, transfer it to a serving dish and pour the sauce over the top, adding a knob of butter and a third of the Parmesan.

Serve individual portions with the remaining grated Parmesan.

Pasta choice fettuccine, tagliatelle

COOK'S TIP
This sauce is usually made with boletus mushrooms in Italy. It can, however, be made equally successfully with any strong-flavoured mushroom. Cultivated button mushrooms are not really suitable as they don't have enough flavour.

Ravioli (page 32) with Tomato and Fresh Basil Sauce (page 37)

Linguine and Tuna Fish Sauce (page 82)

79

KING FERDINANDO'S TAGLIATELLE

(TAGLIATELLE ALLA FERDINANDO II)

575 g/1¼ lb canned tomatoes
1 small onion
100 g/4 oz Parma ham, thickly sliced
small bunch of fresh basil
200 g/7 oz mozzarella cheese
50 g/2 oz butter
salt
50 g/2 oz Parmesan cheese, grated

Prepare the sauce before cooking the tagliatelle.

Crush the tomatoes or blend them briefly in a liquidiser. Finely chop the onion. Cut the Parma ham into thin matchstick-sized pieces. Wash, dry and roughly chop the fresh basil. Dice the mozzarella cheese.

Melt the butter in a frying pan and fry the onion until transparent. Add the tomatoes and salt to taste and simmer gently for approximately 15–20 minutes, until the sauce becomes denser. Add the ham and the chopped basil.

When the pasta is cooked, transfer it to a serving dish and pour the sauce over the top, adding the mozzarella cheese and half the grated Parmesan.

Serve individual portions with extra Parmesan if desired.

Pasta choice tagliatelle

Note: this was the favourite dish of King Ferdinand II who reigned in Naples from 1830–1859. The ingredients are the same, but the method has been brought up to date!

GORGONZOLA SAUCE

(ALLA GORGONZOLA)

200 g/7 oz Gorgonzola cheese
50 g/2 oz butter
6 tablespoons single cream

Make the sauce while the pasta is cooking.

Cut the Gorgonzola into small cubes. Melt the butter and cream in a saucepan and without allowing the cream to boil, add the Gorgonzola. When they have all melted together, stir in a ladle of boiling pasta water.

When the pasta is cooked, transfer it to a serving dish and pour the sauce over the top.

Serve immediately.

Pasta choice pennette, penne, conchiglie, pipe

COOK'S TIP

Danish blue cheese can be substituted for Gorgonzola if preferred.

EGG SAUCE NEAPOLITAN STYLE

(ALL' UOVO FRITTO)

8 eggs
25 g/1 oz lard
salt and freshly ground black pepper
50 g/2 oz pecorino cheese, grated

Lightly fry the eggs in the lard just before the pasta is ready. Sprinkle them with salt.

Divide the freshly cooked pasta between four individual deep dishes. Put two eggs on top of each portion of pasta. Mix well.

Serve with grated pecorino and freshly ground black pepper.

Pasta choice spaghetti, vermicelli

Note: this is a very old Neapolitan recipe and made a one course meal for those who could not afford to buy a second course. It is still eaten today in parts of Naples.

Vodka Sauce

(Alla Vodka)

100 g/4 oz lean cooked ham, thickly sliced
½ wine glass vodka
20 g/¾ oz butter
200 ml/7 fl oz single cream
50 g/2 oz Parmesan cheese, grated

Trim all the fat off the cooked ham. Cut the ham into matchstick-sized pieces, put them in a small bowl and cover them with the vodka. Leave to marinate for about 2 hours.

Towards the end of marinating time, start cooking the pasta.

Put the butter and cream into a saucepan and heat gently without allowing them to boil. Add the ham and the vodka and, stirring all the time, allow the mixture to heat through. Add a ladle of boiling pasta water to thin down the sauce.

When the pasta is cooked, transfer it to a serving dish and pour the sauce over the top, adding half the Parmesan and mix well.

Serve individual portions with the rest of the grated Parmesan.

Pasta choice penne

Note: this sauce is very much in fashion in Italy and even some of the smallest trattorias have it on their menu.

Strawberry Sauce

(Alle Fragole)

225 g/8 oz ripe strawberries
25 g/1 oz butter
1 teaspoon finely grated orange peel
juice of ½ orange
200 ml/7 fl oz single cream
50 g/2 oz Parmesan cheese, grated

Make the sauce before cooking the pasta.

Wash, dry and hull the strawberries and crush them lightly with a fork.

Melt the butter in a frying pan and add the grated orange peel. Sauté gently for a couple of minutes and then add the crushed strawberries and orange juice. Allow to heat through and slowly

add the cream and a tablespoon of grated Parmesan.

While the pasta is cooking, stir a ladle of boiling pasta water into the sauce. Transfer the freshly cooked pasta to a serving dish and pour the sauce over the top.

Serve with the remaining Parmesan.

Pasta choice tagliolini, tagliatelle

Note: fresh fruit sauces are very much in fashion in Italy. You can find pasta with blackberries, blueberries, kiwi fruit and others. This recipe was given to me by one of the owners of the Richelieu restaurant in Monte Porzio Catone, just outside Rome. The restaurant specialises in serving pasta and rice with various fruit sauces.

Lemon Sauce

(Al Limone)

1 large lemon
25 g/1 oz butter
200 ml/7 fl oz single cream
1 tablespoon chopped parsley

Prepare the sauce while the pasta is cooking.

Finely grate the lemon peel, taking great care to grate only the yellow peel and not cut into the white pith. Melt the butter in a saucepan, add the grated lemon peel and cook for 2 minutes, so that the flavour of the lemon mixes with the butter. Do not let the peel fry or the butter turn brown. Add the cream and heat through without allowing the sauce to boil. Add a ladle of pasta water to thin down the sauce.

When the pasta is cooked, transfer it to a serving dish and pour the sauce over the top. Mix well.

Serve individual portions garnished with chopped parsley.

Pasta choice tagliatelle, linguine

Cook's Tip

Be very careful not to cut into the pith of the lemon as the sauce will be very bitter. This sauce has a very fresh flavour and is ideal served before fish or on a hot summer's day.

FISH AND SEAFOOD SAUCES

TUNA FISH SAUCE

(Al Tonno)

Illustrated on page 79

575 g/1¼ lb canned tomatoes
2 cloves garlic
small bunch of parsley
olive oil
salt and freshly ground black pepper
1 (198-g/7-oz) can tuna, drained and flaked

Start making the sauce before cooking the pasta.

Crush the tomatoes or blend them briefly in a liquidiser. Peel and cut each clove of garlic into three or four pieces. Wash and roughly chop the parsley.

Coat the bottom of a large frying pan with olive oil and when it is hot, but not smoking, add the garlic and fry gently until golden. Add the tomatoes, season to taste and simmer gently for approximately 10–15 minutes. Add the tuna.

When the pasta is cooked, transfer it to a serving dish and pour the sauce over the top.

Serve individual portions with chopped parsley.

Pasta choice spaghetti, linguine

COOK'S TIP
The tuna fish sauce should be ready just as you are draining the pasta.

CARTER-STYLE SAUCE

(Alla Carrettiera)

2 cloves garlic
40 g/1½ oz dried boletus mushrooms
1 tablespoon concentrated tomato purée
small bunch of parsley
olive oil
salt and freshly ground black pepper
75 g/3 oz canned tuna, drained and flaked

Prepare the sauce before cooking the spaghetti.

Peel and cut each clove of garlic into three or four pieces. Soak the dried mushrooms in a little hot water until they soften. Drain and chop them into small pieces. Dilute the tomato purée with a ladle of hot water. Roughly chop the parsley.

Coat the bottom of an earthenware casserole with olive oil and gently fry the garlic until golden. Add the chopped mushrooms and fry gently until cooked. Add the diluted tomato purée and allow to simmer for approximately 5 minutes. Salt to taste, then add the tuna fish.

Drain the spaghetti 3–4 minutes before it is perfectly cooked and add it to the sauce in the earthenware casserole. Mix thoroughly and allow to stand for 3–4 minutes before serving to allow the pasta to finish cooking in the sauce.

Serve individual portions with freshly ground black pepper and parsley.

Pasta choice spaghetti

COOK'S TIP
A stock cube dissolved in a ladle of hot water can be used instead of the tomato purée as a variation.

Spaghetti with Baby Clam Sauce (page 87)

CLAM SAUCE

(ALLE VONGOLE)

575 g/1¼ lb canned tomatoes
3 cloves garlic
small bunch of parsley
olive oil
225 g/8 oz frozen shelled clams, thawed
salt and freshly ground black pepper

Make the sauce before cooking the pasta.

Crush the tomatoes or blend them briefly in a liquidiser. Peel and cut each clove of garlic into three or four pieces. Wash, dry and roughly chop the parsley.

Coat the bottom of a large saucepan with olive oil. When the oil is hot, but not smoking, add the garlic and fry gently until golden. Add the tomatoes and simmer for approximately 10 minutes. Add the clams and continue cooking for another 5–10 minutes, until the sauce has become denser. Season to taste.

When the pasta is cooked, transfer it to a serving dish and pour the sauce over the top.

Serve immediately, garnished with the chopped parsley.

Pasta choice spaghetti, vermicelli, linguine

COOK'S TIP
Tinned or bottled clams can be used instead of frozen clams, but drain off the juice before using.

FISHERMAN'S SAUCE

(ALLA PESCATORA)

Illustrated on pages 94 and 95

1 (400-g/14-oz) can tomatoes
2 cloves garlic
small bunch of parsley
400 g/14 oz mixed, cleaned and shelled
molluscs and shellfish, for example,
prawns, clams, mussels, squid, baby
octopus, cuttlefish
olive oil
1 small chilli
salt

Make the sauce before cooking the pasta.

Crush the tomatoes or blend them briefly in a liquidiser. Peel and cut each clove of garlic into three or four pieces. Wash, dry and roughly chop the parsley. Cut the squid, cuttlefish and octopus into small pieces.

Cover the bottom of a large frying pan with olive oil. When the oil is hot, but not smoking, add the garlic and chilli. Fry the garlic until golden and crush the chilli against the bottom of the pan to release its flavour. Add the pieces of squid, cuttlefish and octopus to the hot oil and fry, stirring all the time for about 5–6 minutes. Add the tomatoes and salt to taste and simmer gently for approximately 30 minutes, adding the mussels, clams and prawns 10 minutes before the sauce is ready. While cooking, stir the sauce occasionally and add a little water if necessary to prevent sticking and burning.

When the pasta is cooked, transfer it to a serving dish, add the chopped parsley and pour the sauce over the top.

Serve garnished with more chopped parsley and a few mussel and clam shells if available.

Pasta choice vermicelli, spaghetti, linguine

COOK'S TIP
This sauce can also be served *in bianco*, that is, without the addition of tomatoes. It can also be served with cream. In this case the sauce should be liquidised and the cream added. You will only need half the given ingredients for this version plus a (142-ml/5-fl oz) carton of single cream.

ANCHOVY SAUCE

(ALLE ACCIUGHE)

100 g/4 oz green olives
2 cloves garlic
½ chilli
40 g/1½ oz canned anchovy fillets
150 g/5 oz butter
1 tablespoon chopped parsley

Start preparing the sauce before cooking the pasta.

Stone and chop the olives into small pieces. Peel the garlic and finely chop and crush it, together with the chilli and anchovy fillets.

Melt the butter in an earthenware casserole, add the anchovy mixture and, stirring all the time, allow to fry gently for 4–5 minutes. Add the chopped olives and continue cooking until they become slightly softer and the mixture has become well amalgamated.

Add the drained, freshly cooked pasta and mix well.

Serve immediately, garnished with parsley.

Pasta choice spaghetti, linguine

Note: my husband invented this recipe while convalescing. Left alone at home he decided to experiment with what he could find in a rather empty fridge and kitchen cupboard!

BABY CLAM SAUCE

(ALLE VONGOLE)

Illustrated on page 83

**450 g/1 lb fresh baby clams, in their shells
small bunch of parsley
3 cloves garlic
olive oil
freshly ground black pepper**

Make the sauce before cooking the pasta.

Put the clams in a bowl of water and leave them to stand for 2–3 hours to allow them to expel any sand they may have in their shells. Wash the clams thoroughly by rubbing the shells together between your hands under running water. Wash and roughly chop the parsley. Peel and cut each garlic clove into three or four pieces.

Thickly coat the bottom of a very large saucepan with olive oil. Add the garlic and fry gently until golden. Add the clams and cover the saucepan with a lid. The heat of the oil and the pan will force the clams to open and they will cook in their own juice. Stir the clams occasionally until all of the shells are open. This should take about 10 minutes. The clams will release sea water so it should not be necessary to add salt.

Take half of the clams out of their shells, putting them back in the saucepan and discarding the shells. Add pepper and chopped parsley.

When the pasta is cooked, transfer it to a serving dish and pour the sauce over the top.

Serve immediately, with a dish in the centre of the table for the empty clam shells.

Pasta choice spaghetti, vermicelli

COOK'S TIP

Clams should still be alive when you buy them, otherwise it is not advisable to eat them as they may carry disease. If any of the clams do not open when cooked it is wise to remove them as it usually means that the clam was dead *before* being dropped into the saucepan. Some people prefer to remove almost all the clam shells before serving as they find it difficult to cope with them amongst the spaghetti. Keep a dozen, however, for garnish.

Top: *Linguine with Cream of Prawn Sauce* (page 89)
Bottom: *Tagliolini with Smoked Salmon Sauce* (page 89)

Mussel Sauce

(Alle Cozze)

Illustrated on pages 94 and 95

**450 g / 1 lb fresh mussels
2 cloves garlic
olive oil
350 g / 12 oz canned tomatoes
salt and freshly ground black pepper
2 tablespoons chopped parsley**

Prepare the sauce before cooking the pasta.

Scrub the mussels well to remove any seaweed or other impurities encrusted on the shells. Pull out the byssus (the tuft of silky filament by which the mussels attach themselves to the rocks) from each mussel. Crush the tomatoes or blend them briefly in a liquidiser.

Put the mussels in a very large saucepan over the heat, cover and toss them occasionally to allow all the mussels to open. Take the mussels out of their shells and filter the resulting liquid to remove all the impurities. Throw away any mussels which have not opened as they were probably not fresh before being cooked.

Peel and cut each clove of garlic into three or four pieces.

Cover the bottom of a large frying pan with plenty of olive oil and fry the garlic gently until it is golden. Add the tomatoes and simmer for about 15 minutes, until the sauce becomes denser. Add the strained mussel juice, taste to see if it is necessary to add salt, and continue to simmer for another 10 minutes. Add the mussels, allow them to heat through, then add plenty of freshly ground black pepper and the chopped parsley.

When the pasta is cooked, transfer it to a serving dish and pour the sauce over the top.

Serve immediately, with more pepper if desired. Garnish with a few mussel shells.

Pasta choice vermicelli, spaghetti

Cook's Tip
The mussels should be freshly caught and still be alive. On contact with the heat they will open their shells. If this does not happen, do not use them, as it probably means that they were not fresh when bought. The quantity of canned, or preferably fresh, tomatoes in fish sauces should be just enough to absorb the flavour of the fish and not enough to mask it. The tomatoes should be de-seeded and their watery juice drained off before use to obtain perfect results. Most housewives, however, do not go to this extreme, but simply crush the tomatoes or blend them in a liquidiser. Fish sauces need slightly more oil than meat ones as the fish does not contain any oil of its own.

Caviar Sauce

(Al Caviale)

**50 g / 2 oz butter
200 ml / 7 fl oz single cream
25 g / 1 oz caviar
freshly ground black pepper**

Prepare the sauce while the pasta is cooking.

Melt the butter in a large saucepan, add the cream and heat through to allow the two ingredients to amalgamate well. Add the caviar and a ladle of boiling pasta water and mix well.

When the pasta is cooked, transfer it to a serving dish and pour the sauce over the top.

Serve with freshly ground black pepper if desired.

Pasta choice penne, rigatoni, sedani, conchiglie

Cook's Tip
It is not necessary to use the best Russian caviar for this dish!

CREAM OF PRAWN SAUCE

(ALLA CREMA DI SCAMPI)

Illustrated on pages 86 and 87

**150 g/5 oz prawns, cooked and peeled
25 g/1 oz butter
200 ml/7 fl oz single cream
1 teaspoon concentrated tomato purée
salt
1 tablespoon chopped parsley**

Make the sauce while the pasta is cooking.

Roughly chop the prawns. Melt the butter in a large saucepan, add the cream and the tomato purée and heat through. Add the prawns and salt to taste. Stir in a ladle of pasta water.

When the pasta is cooked, transfer it to a serving dish and pour the sauce over the top.

Serve individual portions garnished with chopped parsley.

Pasta choice linguine, fettuccine, tagliolini

COOK'S TIP

A chilli may be added if liked. Add while melting the butter and rub it against the bottom of the pan to release its flavour. Remove the chilli before serving the sauce.

SMOKED SALMON SAUCE

(AL SALMONE)

Illustrated on pages 86 and 87

**50 g/2 oz smoked salmon
25 g/1 oz butter
200 ml/7 fl oz single cream
salt
1 tablespoon grated Parmesan cheese**

Prepare the sauce while the pasta is cooking, or just before if fresh pasta is being used.

Cut the salmon into short, thin strips. Melt the butter in a large saucepan and add the cream. Heat through and add the smoked salmon and salt to taste. Stir in a ladle of boiling pasta water.

When the pasta is cooked, transfer it to a serving dish and pour the sauce over the top, adding the grated cheese and mixing thoroughly.

Serve immediately as it is.

Pasta choice tagliolini, linguine

COOK'S TIP

Cheese is not usually used in fish sauces, but this is one of the exceptions!

Note: there is no need to go to great expense in buying smoked salmon. Look out for salmon offcuts in delicatessens, or buy frozen salmon offcuts in a supermarket.

MAKING TORTELLINI

1   Cut the chicken, veal and pork into small pieces and fry gently until golden brown.

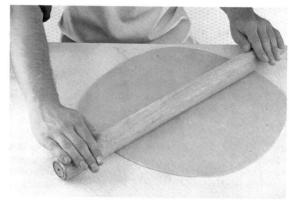

2   Make the pasta dough as for fettuccine (see page 28). Roll it out into one large circle.

3   Cut the circle in half. Fold one half over to keep it moist while you cut the other half into 2.5-cm/1-in squares with a pastry wheel.

4   Put a small amount of stuffing in the centre of each square and fold the pasta over to make a triangle, pinching the edges together well.

5   Hold the triangle between the thumb and forefinger of your left hand and turn the point down towards you, while pinching the two ends of the triangle together firmly as you slide the tortellino off the tip of your finger.

6   Cook the tortellini in fast boiling salted water. Lift them out of the water with a draining spoon and drain thoroughly in a colander before transferring them to a serving dish (opposite).

TORTELLINI

Illustrated on pages 90 and 91

STUFFING
75 g/3 oz chicken or turkey breast
75 g/3 oz veal
75 g/3 oz lean pork
25 g/1 oz butter
1 clove
25 g/1 oz Parma ham
salt and freshly ground black pepper
brandy
1 egg
40 g/1$\frac{1}{2}$ oz Parmesan cheese, grated
$\frac{1}{4}$ teaspoon grated nutmeg

PASTA
3 eggs
300 g/11 oz strong plain flour plus extra for working

Cut the chicken, veal and pork into small pieces and fry them gently in the butter with the clove, until golden brown. Add the Parma ham, cut into small pieces, just before all the other meat is ready. Salt to taste. Sprinkle the meat with a few drops of brandy and allow it to evaporate. Remove the clove.

Leave the meat to cool, then finely chop it together until it resembles minced meat. Put it into a bowl and add the egg, grated cheese, grated nutmeg, freshly ground black pepper and salt to taste. Mix all the ingredients together thoroughly with a fork and leave the mixture to stand for several hours in a cool, dry place before using.

Make the pasta dough as for fettuccine, but rolling it out into one large circle, and without leaving it to dry.

Fold one half of the circle over to help keep it moist while you are cutting the other half into squares of approximately 2.5 cm/1 in with a pastry wheel. Pile up the cut squares on top of each other to prevent them from drying out while you are shaping the tortellini.

Put a small amount of stuffing in the centre of each square and fold the pasta over to make a triangle, pinching the edges together well. If the pasta is too dry you can wet the points of the triangle slightly with a drop of water. Hold the triangle between the thumb and forefinger of your left hand and turn the point down towards you at the same time as turning the two ends of the triangle around your finger and pinching them well together as you slide the tortellino off the tip of your finger. The 'point' of the tortellino should be slightly higher than the 'bulge'. Lay the finished tortellini out on a tray which has been covered with a tea-towel.

Drop the tortellini into a large open pan of fast boiling salted water, leaving them for 3–4 minutes after the water has come back to a fast boil. Lift them out of the water with a draining spoon and drain thoroughly in a colander before putting them into the serving dish.

Serve immediately with your favourite sauce.

Sauce choice butter, cream, ragoût

COOK'S TIP
Best made, cooked and served immediately. They will keep in the refrigerator until the next day, or can be frozen. Tortellini can also be cooked and served in consommé. The stuffing can be made in larger batches, frozen and used as needed, but do not freeze tortellini made from frozen stuffing!

BAKED PASTA

PASTA BAKED MY STYLE

(A MODO MIO)

200 g/7 oz button mushrooms
75 g/3 oz butter
salt and pepper
200 g/7 oz small frozen peas
1 (300-g/11-oz) mozzarella cheese
200 g/7 oz lean cooked ham
50 g/2 oz plain flour
750 ml/1¼ pints milk
100 g/4 oz Parmesan cheese, grated
350 g/12 oz pasta

Wash and thinly slice the mushrooms. Melt 25 g/ 1 oz of the butter in a frying pan and gently fry the mushrooms until tender. Add salt to taste. Cook the frozen peas in boiling salted water, drain and reserve them with the mushrooms. Cut the mozzarella cheese into small cubes. Trim all the fat off the ham and cut into matchstick-sized pieces.

Melt the remaining butter in a small saucepan and stir in the flour, eliminating any lumps. Cook the resulting roux or paste for a few minutes over a low heat, without allowing it to change colour, until it resembles a honeycomb. Take the pan off the heat and slowly beat in the milk, making sure there are no lumps. Slowly bring the sauce to the boil, stirring all the time until it thickens. It should be of a pouring consistency. Add three-quarters of the grated Parmesan and season to taste.

Cook the pasta in boiling salted water and drain when it is three-quarters cooked. Mix the pasta with a ladle of the sauce.

Spread a thin layer of white sauce on the bottom of an ovenproof dish and fill with layers of pasta, mozzarella, peas, ham and mushrooms and white sauce, finishing with a layer of white sauce. Sprinkle the remaining Parmesan over the top.

Bake at the top of a moderately hot oven (200 C, 400 F, gas 6) for approximately 15–20 minutes, until the top is golden.

Serve with extra grated Parmesan if desired.

Pasta choice rigatoni, penne, sedani

COOK'S TIP
You can create your own variations of this dish by adding or subtracting ingredients. Select from the following: deseeded, chopped and fried red or green peppers, chopped and fried onion, crushed cloves of garlic, canned or defrosted frozen sweetcorn, lightly cooked cut French beans, peeled, deseeded and chopped tomatoes. Instead of ham, try crispy fried bacon cubes, chopped salami, sliced cooked sausage, or other cooked meats. If you do not have any Parmesan, grated Cheddar or any other cheese can be substituted. If you like, include herbs; for example, basil, oregano, or parsley will all contribute an excellent flavour to the dish.

MACCHERONI AL GRATIN

100 g/4 oz butter
50 g/2 oz plain flour
750 ml/$1\frac{1}{4}$ pints milk
100 g/4 oz Parmesan cheese, grated
salt and freshly ground black pepper
$\frac{1}{2}$ teaspoon grated nutmeg
350 g/12 oz pasta
2 tablespoons fine breadcrumbs

Melt half of the butter in a small saucepan and stir in the flour, eliminating any lumps. Cook the resulting roux for a few minutes over a low heat, without allowing it to change colour, until it resembles a honeycomb. Take the pan off the heat and very slowly beat in the milk, making sure there are no lumps. Slowly bring the sauce to the boil, stirring all the time until it thickens. It should be of a pouring consistency. Add three-quarters of the grated cheese, stir well, season to taste and add the grated nutmeg.

Cook the pasta in boiling salted water and drain when it is three-quarters cooked.

Mix three-quarters of the sauce with the pasta and pour into an ovenproof dish. Pour the rest of the cheese sauce over the pasta and sprinkle the top with the remaining Parmesan and the breadcrumbs. Cut the butter into small knobs and distribute evenly over the top of the dish.

Bake in the middle of a moderately hot oven (200 C, 400 F, gas 6) for approximately 20 minutes, until a golden brown crust has formed.

Serve with extra grated Parmesan if desired.

Pasta choice rigatoni, sedani, penne, tortiglioni

COOK'S TIP
The dish can be browned further under the grill if the pasta is ready before a crust has formed. This dish is a great success at parties if baked in a shortcrust pastry flan case.

Top: *Spaghetti with Mussel Sauce (page 88)*
Bottom: *Linguine with Fisherman's Sauce (page 84)*

CLASSIC LASAGNE

(LASAGNE CLASSICHE)

1 quantity Bolognese Sauce (page 56)

COATING WHITE SAUCE
50 g/2 oz butter
50 g/2 oz plain flour
750 ml/1¼ pints milk
salt and pepper
1 tablespoon olive oil

PASTA
300 g/11 oz lasagne, plain green or white strips, or a mixture
150 g/5 oz Parmesan cheese, grated

Prepare the Bolognese sauce the day before serving the lasagne and reheat it while cooking the pasta.

Melt the butter in a small saucepan and stir in the flour, eliminating any lumps. Cook the resulting roux or paste for a few minutes, without allowing it to change colour, until it resembles a honeycomb. Take the pan off the heat and very slowly beat in the milk making sure that there are no lumps. Slowly bring the sauce to the boil, stirring all the time, until it thickens. It should be of a pouring consistency. Season to taste. If you are not ready to use the sauce, place a circle of wet greaseproof paper on the surface to prevent a skin from forming.

Add the olive oil to the salted water in which the pasta is to be cooked to prevent the strips of pasta from sticking together. Drop the pasta strips into the fast boiling water one by one, arranging them around the sides of the pan so that they will cook separately. As soon as the lasagne is very *al dente*, pour it out gently into the colander and rinse it with cold water to halt the cooking process. Taking care not to tear the strips lay them out on a clean, dry tea-towel.

Spread a thin layer of Bolognese sauce over the bottom of the ovenproof dish. Cover this length-ways with pasta strips, overlapping them slightly so that there are no gaps in the layer. Pour a layer of Bolognese sauce over the pasta, followed by a layer of white sauce sprinkled with grated Parmesan. Continue making layers in this way, but placing the pasta strips widthways, every alternate layer. If the strips are sometimes longer than the dish, fold them over the top of the layers of sauces before starting your next layer of pasta. Top the dish with a thick layer of white sauce making sure that all the pasta is well covered and sprinkle the top with grated Parmesan.

Bake in a moderately hot oven (200 C, 400 F, gas 6) for about 30 minutes, until the top layer is golden.

Serve when the lasagne has cooled down a little. Lasagne is delicious even when eaten the day after!

COOK'S TIP
If using home-made lasagne, they must be cooked one at a time in boiling water as they are much more delicate than the dried variety.

Note: this traditional recipe comes from central northern Italy in the Emilia-Romagna region.

NEAPOLITAN LASAGNE

(LASAGNE ALLA NAPOLETANA)

Illustrated on page 98

1½ quantities Ragoût Sauce (page 57)
50 g/2 oz stale bread
150 g/5 oz lean beef, finely minced
2 eggs
1 teaspoon finely grated lemon peel
50 g/2 oz Parmesan cheese, grated
salt
plain flour
olive oil
200 g/7 oz provola cheese (smoked mozzarella)
200 g/7 oz mozzarella cheese
3 hard-boiled eggs
300 g/11 oz lasagne, plain or frilly white strips
300 g/11 oz ricotta cheese

Prepare the ragoût sauce ideally the day before and reheat while cooking the pasta.

Soak the stale bread in warm water until it softens. Squeeze it out well to eliminate the water and crumble the soaked bread between your fingers. Put the minced beef into a bowl, add the bread, eggs, lemon peel, grated Parmesan and salt to taste and mix together well. Shape the mixture into mini-meatballs the size of marbles. Roll them in flour and fry them gently in olive oil until cooked through and golden brown. Drain them well on kitchen paper.

Peel the smoked mozzarella cheese and cut it, with the mozzarella, into small cubes of about 1 cm/½ in. Cut the hard-boiled eggs into thin slices.

Add 1 tablespoon of olive oil to the salted water in which the pasta is to be cooked to prevent the strips of pasta from sticking together. Drop the pasta strips one by one into the fast boiling water, arranging them around the sides of the pan so that they cook separately.

Take a ladle of pasta water and mix it with the ricotta cheese in a basin, adding a ladle of hot ragoût sauce. As soon as the lasagne is *al dente* pour it out gently into the colander and rinse it with cold water to halt the cooking process. Taking care not to tear the strips, lay them out on a clean, dry tea-towel.

Cover the bottom of the ovenproof dish with a thin layer of ragoût sauce and start filling it with lasagne, ragoût sauce, ricotta sauce, diced cheeses, mini-meatballs and hard-boiled eggs. The pasta strips should overlap slightly to avoid gaps and they should be placed lengthways and widthways on alternate layers. Continue with the layers until you have used up all the ingredients, finishing with a top layer of ragoût sauce covered with diced cheeses and decorated with a few meatballs. The pasta should be completely covered with sauce so that the edges do not burn.

Bake in the middle of a moderately hot oven (200 C, 400 F, gas 6) for approximately 30 minutes, or until the top is golden brown. The dish can be prepared in advance and heated through before serving.

Serve when the lasagne has cooled down a little. It is best eaten just warm.

COOK'S TIP
In Naples strips of pasta about 40 cm/16 in long are used to line the baking tin, with their edges hanging over the sides. These ends are then folded over the top when all the layers have been completed to seal the 'pie'. Traditional Neapolitan lasagne is always made in a round baking tin and the lasagne is layered in a criss-cross fashion. This recipe is not recommended for beginners, so try it out first on your family before inviting guests!

CANNELLONI

Illustrated on pages 102 and 103

Cannelloni can really be filled with anything you choose. You can amuse yourself inventing new fillings, but the basic ingredient of all cannelloni except those with ricotta cheese, is the white sauce which binds the filling ingredients together.

BINDING WHITE SAUCE
50 g/2 oz butter
40 g/1½ oz plain flour
250 ml/8 fl oz milk
salt
grated nutmeg

Melt the butter in a small saucepan and stir in the flour slowly to avoid lumps forming. Allow the mixture to cook over a low heat, without changing colour, until it resembles a honeycomb. Heat the milk in another saucepan and when it is boiling stir it into the butter and flour, taking the pan off the heat. Beat the sauce for two or three minutes until it becomes thick and glossy. Add the salt and grated nutmeg to taste. Add the chosen filling ingredients. Allow to stand for a couple of hours for the flavours to amalgamate.

Prepare the coating sauce which can be either Tomato (page 36), Tomato and Fresh Basil (page 37), Bolognese (page 56), or Ragoût (page 57), depending on the type of filling in the cannelloni.

If a coating white sauce is preferred, follow the recipe given on page 96.

Cook the cannelloni pasta pieces in boiling salted water one or two at a time and lift them out while they are still *al dente*. Put them to drain on a clean, dry tea-towel.

Divide the filling between the pasta pieces and roll them up, with the filling in the middle, to form cannelloni.

Spread a little sauce over the bottom of a rectangular ovenproof dish, and arrange the cannelloni in rows. Coat the cannelloni with the chosen sauce and/or white sauce, and sprinkle with grated Parmesan.

Bake at the top of a moderately hot oven (200 C, 400 F, gas 6) until heated through, about 20 minutes, and the cheese has melted and turned golden brown.

Opposite: *Neapolitan Lasagne (page 97)*

CANNELLONI WITH PEAS, MUSHROOMS AND COOKED HAM

(CON PISELLI, FUNGHI E PROSCIUTTO)

FILLING
100 g/4 oz small frozen peas
200 g/7 oz mushrooms
25 g/1 oz butter
200 g/7 oz lean cooked ham
1 egg plus 1 egg yolk
2 tablespoons Binding White Sauce (page 99)
50 g/2 oz Parmesan cheese, grated
grated nutmeg
salt and freshly ground black pepper

PASTA
12 pieces pasta for cannelloni, cooked

SAUCE
500 ml/17 fl oz Coating White Sauce (page 96)
25 g/1 oz Parmesan cheese, grated

Cook the peas in boiling salted water and drain well. Wash, peel and thinly slice the mushrooms and fry them gently in the butter until tender. Trim all the fat off the cooked ham and chop the meat into very small pieces.

Beat the egg and egg yolk into the binding white sauce, add the grated cheese, nutmeg, peas, ham and mushrooms. Season to taste and mix well.

Fill the cannelloni, place them in an ovenproof dish and coat them with the white sauce. Sprinkle with the grated Parmesan.

Bake at the top of a moderately hot oven (200 C, 400 F, gas 6) for approximately 20 minutes, until the top is golden brown.

COOK'S TIP

Pieces of leftover cold meats, for example, chicken from the Sunday roast, can be substituted for the cooked ham.

MEAT-FILLED CANNELLONI

(CON LA CARNE)

FILLING
25 g/1 oz butter
150 g/5 oz lean minced beef
100 g/4 oz lean minced pork
100 g/4 oz minced chicken or turkey breast
1 clove
brandy
salt and freshly ground black pepper
1 egg plus 1 egg yolk
2 tablespoons Binding White Sauce (page 99)
50 g/2 oz Parmesan cheese, grated
grated nutmeg

PASTA
12 pieces of pasta for cannelloni, cooked

SAUCE
1 quantity Ragoût (page 57) or Bolognese (page 56)
1 quantity Coating White Sauce (page 96)
25 g/1 oz Parmesan cheese, grated

Melt the butter in a frying pan and gently fry the minced meats with the clove until they are golden brown. Sprinkle them with a little brandy and allow it to evaporate. Season to taste and remove the clove. Beat the egg and egg yolk into the binding white sauce, add the grated Parmesan, nutmeg and the minced meats.

Fill the cannelloni, place them in an ovenproof dish and coat them with the meat sauce, then the white sauce. Sprinkle them with the grated Parmesan.

Bake at the top of a moderately hot oven (200 C, 400 F, gas 6) for approximately 20 minutes until the top is golden brown.

Serve immediately with more grated Parmesan if desired.

COOK'S TIP

Different minced meats can be used and a little cooked ham can be added if desired.

CANNELLONI WITH RICOTTA AND SPINACH

(CON RICOTTA E SPINACI)

FILLING
300 g / 11 oz frozen whole-leaf spinach
400 g / 14 oz ricotta cheese
50 g / 2 oz Parmesan cheese, grated
1 egg plus 1 egg yolk
salt
grated nutmeg

PASTA
12 pieces of pasta for cannelloni, cooked

SAUCE
1 quantity Tomato and Fresh Basil (page 37)
25 g / 1 oz Parmesan cheese, grated

Cook the spinach in boiling salted water and drain well, squeezing out most of the water. Finely chop the spinach or blend it briefly in a liquidiser. Pass the ricotta cheese through a sieve and add the chopped spinach, grated Parmesan, egg, egg yolk, salt and grated nutmeg. Mix the ingredients together thoroughly.

Fill the cannelloni, place them in an ovenproof dish, coat them with the tomato sauce and sprinkle with the grated Parmesan.

Bake at the top of a moderately hot oven (200 C, 400 F, gas 6) for approximately 20 minutes, until the cannelloni have heated through and the cheese is golden.

COOK'S TIP
The sauce is best made with fresh tomatoes. Ricotta is a fresh, unsalted curd cheese which can easily be made at home if it cannot be found in the shops. (See recipe on page 73.)

GRANDMOTHER MARY'S BAKED PASTA

(Alla Nonna Maria)

small bunch of fresh basil
800 g/1¾ lb juicy, ripe tomatoes
350 g/12 oz pasta
salt
50 g/2 oz butter
grated Parmesan cheese to serve (optional)

Wash, dry and tear the basil leaves into small pieces. Cut the tomatoes in half across the middle and, in a tall casserole, form layers of tomatoes and pasta, seasoning each layer of tomatoes with salt and adding basil and flakes of butter. Start with a layer of tomato halves then pasta, then more tomato halves turned upside down. Repeat this order until all the pasta and tomatoes have been used. Press the top layer of tomatoes (skins upwards) down well. The juice from the tomatoes should come at least three-quarters of the way up the sides of the casserole. If the juice is not sufficient add a little water.

Bake in the middle of a moderately hot oven (200 C, 400 F, gas 6) for about 45 minutes, until the pasta is cooked and has absorbed all the excess juice. Cover the casserole with a lid for the first 30 minutes.

Serve with grated Parmesan if desired.

Pasta choice penne, sedani

COOK'S TIP
Do not attempt to make this dish if the tomatoes are not really juicy or the pasta will not cook properly.

Note: this is a very old recipe given to me by a friend who remembers the dish as her grandmother used to make it. It was originally baked in a tall saucepan, without handles, in the oven.

Top: *Cannelloni (pages 99–101)*
Bottom: *Sicilian-style Baked Pasta (page 104)*

Sicilian-style Baked Pasta

(Alla Siciliana)

Illustrated on pages 102 and 103

575 g/1¼ lb canned tomatoes
1 clove garlic
1 medium onion
olive oil
150 g/5 oz lean minced beef
1 glass dry white wine
salt and coarse sea salt
2 large aubergines
1 (300-g/11-oz) mozzarella cheese
350 g/12 oz pasta
100 g/4 oz Parmesan cheese, grated

Crush the tomatoes or blend them briefly in a liquidiser. Peel the clove of garlic. Finely chop the onion.

Coat the bottom of a large saucepan with olive oil and gently fry the onion until transparent and the garlic until golden. Add the minced beef and fry gently, stirring all the time to prevent the meat from sticking together. Add the wine and allow it to evaporate. Add the tomatoes and salt to taste and simmer gently for about 30–40 minutes, until the sauce becomes denser and darker. Remove the clove of garlic.

Wash, dry and, without peeling them, thinly slice the aubergines either lengthways or into circles, depending on their size. Layer the slices of aubergine with a little coarse sea salt in a colander, put a weight on the top, press down well and leave for about 30 minutes to allow the salt to draw the bitterness out of them. Rinse off all the salt under running water and squeeze out the aubergines well. Gently fry the slices of aubergine in olive oil and drain them on kitchen paper.

Cut the mozzarella cheese into thin slices.

Cook the pasta in boiling salted water and drain well when it is three-quarters cooked. Mix the pasta with a ladle of meat sauce.

Spread a thin layer of meat sauce on the bottom of an ovenproof dish and form layers of pasta, sauce, aubergines, mozzarella and grated Parmesan in this order twice, finishing with the mozzarella and Parmesan.

Bake in the middle of a moderately hot oven (200 C, 400 F, gas 6) for about 20 minutes, until the mozzarella has melted and the top is golden.

Pasta choice penne, rigatoni, sedani

Cook's Tip

The meat sauce can be made the day before, chilled overnight and reheated while cooking the pasta. Delicious flavours will develop from the various ingredients. Alternatively, this is an excellent dish to make up to several weeks in advance and freeze. You may choose to make and freeze the whole dish, or just the meat sauce.

Serve freshly baked and bubbling hot. An accompaniment of warm crusty bread offers an interesting contrast in texture to this juicy pasta dish.

TAGLIOLINI PIE

(PASTICCIO DI TAGLIOLINI)

FILLING
150 g/5 oz button mushrooms
50 g/2 oz butter
salt and freshly ground black pepper
150 g/5 oz small frozen peas
150 g/5 oz lean cooked ham
25 g/1 oz plain flour
500 ml/17 fl oz milk
50 g/2 oz Parmesan cheese, grated
300 g/11 oz tagliolini

PASTRY CRUST
400 g/14 oz plain flour
200 g/7 oz margarine
about 3 tablespoons cold water
$\frac{1}{2}$ teaspoon salt
a little beaten egg to glaze

Wash and thinly slice the mushrooms. Melt half the butter in the frying pan and gently fry the mushrooms until tender. Add salt to taste. Cook the peas in boiling salted water, drain and reserve them with the mushrooms. Trim all the fat off the cooked ham and cut it into small pieces of approximately 1 cm/$\frac{1}{2}$ in.

Melt the remaining butter in a small saucepan and stir in the flour. Cook the resulting roux or paste for a few minutes over a low heat, without allowing it to change colour, until it resembles a honeycomb. Take the pan off the heat and slowly beat in the milk. Bring the sauce to the boil, stirring all the time until it thickens. Add the grated Parmesan, the peas, the ham, mushrooms and seasoning to taste.

Cook the pasta in boiling salted water and drain when it is three-quarters cooked. Mix the pasta with the sauce and allow to stand.

To make the pastry, place the flour and salt in a bowl. Add the margarine and rub in lightly with the fingertips until the mixture resembles fine breadcrumbs. Sprinkle over the water and mix, using a round-bladed knife, until the mixture begins to bind together to form a dough. Knead together very lightly, then divide the dough in two. Roll out one portion of pastry and use it to line a flan dish, about 30 cm/12 in. in diameter. Roll out the remaining pastry for the lid. Cut out one or two pastry leaves for decorating the top of the pie.

Pour the pasta and sauce into the pastry case, put on the lid and seal the edges well. Make a slit in the top of the pie to allow the steam to escape, decorate with the pastry leaves and glaze with the beaten egg.

Bake in the middle of a moderately hot oven (200 C, 400 F, gas 6) for approximately 35 minutes until the pastry is cooked and the top is golden brown.

Pasta choice tagliolini, tagliatelle, fettuccine, paglia e fieno (straw and hay)

COOK'S TIP
If you use paglia e fieno – the green and white pasta – you get a pleasing colour combination when cutting the individual slices. A variation of the filling can be made by substituting smoked salmon offcuts from a delicatessen, or frozen smoked salmon offcuts for the peas, ham and mushrooms.

MACCHERONI PIE
(PASTICCIO DI MACCHERONI)

Illustrated opposite

FILLING
1 quantity Bolognese Sauce (page 56)
½ teaspoon grated nutmeg
2 tablespoons Binding White Sauce (page 99)
300 g/11 oz pasta

PASTRY CRUST
200 g/7 oz butter
200 g/7 oz caster sugar
6 egg yolks
about 300 g/11 oz plain flour
pinch of salt

GLAZE
beaten egg

Make the Bolognese sauce, preferably the day before, using only 400 g/14 oz canned tomatoes.

Add the nutmeg to the binding white sauce.

Cook the pasta in boiling salted water and drain just before it is completely cooked through.

Mix the pasta with the meat sauce and 2 tablespoons of binding white sauce and leave to stand for approximately 2 hours to allow the pasta to absorb the sauce well.

Make the pastry crust by mixing the butter, sugar and egg yolks together and kneading in the flour and salt until you have a very soft dough which will be quite sticky. Use a little more flour if necessary.

Grease a round, shallow baking tin or pyrex flan dish about 28 cm/11 in. in diameter. Put approximately two-thirds of the pastry into the baking tin and, using the heel of your palm and your fingers, gently flatten the pastry and push it outwards from the centre until it has lined the tin. (It will be too soft and sticky to roll out). Put the remaining third of the pastry on to a well floured working surface and, using your hands as before, form a flat circle large enough to cover the top of the pie.

Put the pasta and sauce into the pie case and press it down really well. Cover the pie with the pastry circle, sealing the edges well. Make a small slit in the centre of the lid to allow the steam to escape.

Maccheroni Pie

Bake in a moderately hot oven (200 C, 400 F, gas 6) for about 30 minutes until the pastry is cooked. Glaze the top with a little beaten egg 10 minutes before the pie is ready and it will turn a shiny golden brown.

Serve when just warm, or even when cold.

Pasta choice rigatoni, sedani, tortiglioni

COOK'S TIP
This is a very old traditional recipe from Emilia-Romagna. The pastry is very sweet and its typical sweet-savoury combination is not to everyone's taste. These pies, made in individual portions, used to be eaten piping hot from the bakers, early in the morning for breakfast!

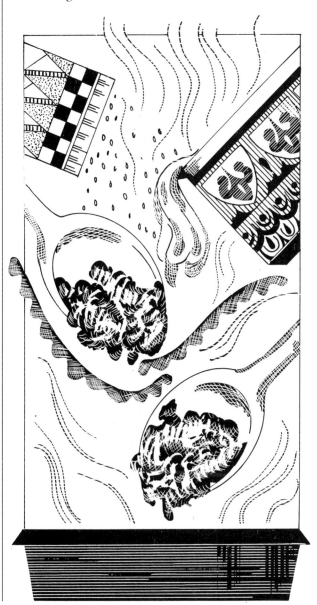

PASTA SOUPS – THICK AND THIN

PASTA AND POTATO SOUP

(PASTA E PATATE)

**2 cloves garlic
1 stick celery
4 medium potatoes
small bunch of parsley
olive oil
salt
50 g/2 oz pasta per person**

Prepare the soup before cooking the pasta.

Peel and cut each clove of garlic into three or four pieces. Chop the celery into small pieces. Peel and dice the potatoes. Wash and roughly chop the parsley.

Coat the bottom of a large saucepan with olive oil, add the garlic and fry gently until golden. Add the celery, potatoes, a generous teaspoon of parsley and just enough water to cover the contents of the saucepan. Add salt to taste and simmer gently for about 20 minutes, until the potatoes are cooked and just beginning to break up and thicken the liquid. Stir occasionally to prevent from sticking and add water if necessary.

Drain the pasta a couple of minutes before it is perfectly cooked and add it to the soup. Mix thoroughly, adding a little pasta water if needed to keep the mixture moist. Leave to stand for about 5 minutes before serving, to allow the pasta to finish cooking in the heat of the potato soup.

Serve garnished with chopped parsley.

Pasta choice pasta mista, tubetti, occhi di lupo, ditali

Note: this dish originates in the south of Italy and is often prepared in the home. It can be rarely found on restaurant menus.

PASTA AND PEA SOUP

(PASTA E PISELLI)

2 medium onions
1 rindless rasher lean streaky bacon
olive oil
1 (454-g/1-lb) packet frozen peas
salt
50 g/2 oz pasta per person

Make the soup before cooking the pasta.

Finely chop the onions. Chop the bacon rasher into small pieces of about 1 cm/$\frac{1}{2}$ in.

Coat the bottom of a large saucepan with olive oil, add the bacon and onion and fry gently until the bacon becomes crispy and the onion transparent. Add the frozen peas and just enough water to cover the contents of the pan and simmer gently, adding salt to taste, until the peas are tender. Extra water may be needed during the cooking, which takes approximately 20 minutes.

When the pasta is cooked add it to the soup. Serve with Parmesan cheese if desired.

Pasta choice tubetti, ditali, occhi di lupo

COOK'S TIP

A chicken stock cube can be added to the peas while cooking instead of the salt, but remember the monosodium glutamate it contains!

Broken pieces of spaghetti can be used instead of the recommended pasta shapes. The tubetti family are ideal, however, as the peas can hide inside the pasta.

PASTA AND BEAN SOUP

(PASTA E FAGIOLI IN BIANCO)

2 cloves garlic
2 sticks celery
1 small potato, peeled
olive oil
salt and freshly ground black pepper
2 (425-g/15-oz) cans cannellini beans
50 g/2 oz pasta per person

Make the sauce before cooking the pasta.

Peel and cut each clove of garlic into three or four pieces. Chop the celery and potato into small pieces of about 1 cm/$\frac{1}{2}$ in.

Coat the base of a large saucepan with olive oil and when hot, but not smoking, add the garlic and fry until golden. Add the celery, potato, salt to taste and a glass of water and simmer gently. Stir frequently, adding more water if necessary to prevent sticking and cook for approximately 20 minutes, until the celery and potato are soft. Add the beans and the juice from the cans and heat through. Adjust the consistency by adding more water if desired.

Drain the pasta a couple of minutes before it is perfectly cooked, and add it to the soup. Mix thoroughly, adding plenty of freshly ground black pepper and allow to stand for about 5 minutes before serving, so that the pasta finishes cooking in the heat of the bean sauce and absorbs the flavour.

Serve individual portions with extra pepper if desired.

Pasta choice ditali, pasta mista, occhi di lupo, tubetti

COOK'S TIP

Some people prefer to add a tomato with the celery and potato to give the soup some colour.

PASTA AND LENTIL SOUP

(PASTA E LENTICCHIE)

Illustrated opposite

225 g/8 oz small dried lentils
salt
2 cloves garlic
175 g/6 oz canned tomatoes
small bunch of parsley
olive oil
50 g/2 oz pasta per person

The lentils can be cooked and the sauce made the day before and the pasta added before serving.

Check the lentils, if bought loose, for small stones and foreign bodies. Put them into a large bowl and add enough water to come a good 5 cm/ 2 in above the level of the lentils. Leave to soak for about 10–12 hours.

Drain the water off the lentils and put them into a large saucepan, adding enough water to come about 5 cm/2 in above the level of the lentils. Add 1 rounded teaspoon of salt, bring to the boil and simmer until the lentils are three-quarters cooked. The time will vary considerably, depending on the quality and type of lentils used.

While the lentils are cooking, peel the garlic and cut each clove into three or four pieces. Crush the tomatoes or blend them briefly in a liquidiser. Wash and roughly chop the parsley.

Coat the base of a saucepan with olive oil and gently fry the garlic until golden. Add the tomatoes and half the parsley and simmer gently for approximately 10 minutes, until the tomato is cooked, adding salt to taste.

When the lentils are ready, pour the sauce into the lentils, add a little water if necessary, enough to cook the pasta, then bring to the boil and add the pasta. Cook according to the type of pasta used.

Serve individual portions garnished with chopped parsley.

Pasta choice tubetti, occhi di lupo, ditalini, pasta mista

COOK'S TIP
This dish can be served either as a fairly liquid soup or as a thicker mixture, depending on one's taste and the quantity of water added.

PASTA AND CHICK PEA SOUP

(PASTA E CECI)

350 g/12 oz dried chick peas
1 teaspoon bicarbonate of soda
50 g/2 oz spinach
1 stick celery
1 medium onion
6 tablespoons olive oil
3 canned tomatoes
salt
50 g/2 oz pasta per person

The chick peas can be cooked in advance and the pasta added just before serving.

Put the chick peas in a large bowl and add enough water to come at least 5 cm/2 in above their level. Add the bicarbonate of soda and leave to soak overnight.

Drain the liquid off the chick peas, keeping a glassful to use during the cooking. Drop the chick peas into boiling water, adding the glass of soaking water and boil until three-quarters cooked.

Chop the spinach, celery and onion together.

Heat the oil in a large saucepan and gently fry the chopped vegetables until tender, adding the tomatoes and salt to taste. Add the chick peas and enough of the water in which they were boiled to cook the pasta. Bring to the boil, add the pasta and simmer until the pasta is cooked.

Serve immediately, as it is.

Pasta choice pasta mista, tubetti, occhi di lupo

COOK'S TIP
The bicarbonate of soda is used to help soften the chick peas and to revive their golden yellow colour which they lose when they are dried. Exact quantities of water have not been given, as this may vary according to the quality of the chick peas used.

Top: *Small Pasta in Consommé (page 112)*
Bottom: *Pasta and Lentil Soup*

SMALL PASTA IN CONSOMMÉ

(PASTINA IN BRODO)

Illustrated on page 110

2 carrots
1 stick celery
1 medium potato
1 ripe tomato
1 medium onion
small bunch of parsley
$\frac{1}{2}$ chicken or boiling fowl
400 g/14 oz brisket of beef
1 teaspoon salt
50 g/2 oz pasta per person
65 g/2$\frac{1}{2}$ oz Parmesan cheese, grated

Make the consommé the day before serving.

Scrub the carrots, celery and potato. Top and tail the carrots, cut the celery stick, the tomato, onion and potato into two. Wash the parsley and rinse the chicken and beef.

Put all the above ingredients in a large saucepan and add enough water to amply cover the contents and to come three-quarters of the way up the sides of the pan. Add the salt. Bring the water to the boil and simmer very slowly for about 3 hours, topping up with more water if the level falls below that of the meat. (A pressure cooker will reduce the cooking time to 45 minutes.)

Remove the meat from the pan and strain the consommé through a fine sieve. Allow it to stand overnight and when completely cold, skim the fat off the surface. Bring the strained consommé to the boil and add the pasta. Cook according to the type of pasta used. Add a little cold water.

Serve with grated Parmesan.

Pasta choice all types of very small pasta: anellini, capellini, lancette, pepe, quadretti, stelline, or tortellini or spaghetti which has been broken into short lengths.

COOK'S TIP

The chicken can be served as a second course with a little of the consommé and the boiled vegetables. The brisket can be made into a salad by trimming off all the fat, breaking the meat into thin strands and dressing it with oil, lemon juice, salt and chopped parsley. The cold water is added to the consommé to cool it down slightly so that the grated cheese, when added, does not melt and stick to the bottom of the dish.

STRACCIATELLA

3 eggs
50 g/2 oz Parmesan cheese, grated
salt
150 g/5 oz pasta
1 litre/1¾ pints consommé

Beat the eggs with half the grated cheese and a little salt to taste. Cook the pasta in boiling consommé and when it is ready, stirring all the time, add the beaten egg. The egg will set on contact with the boiling liquid, forming very thin strands of scrambled egg, which look like 'rags'.

Serve immediately, with the remaining Parmesan.

Pasta choice stelline, pepe, or any of the very small pasta.

COOK'S TIP

This is a Roman dish and is often made by mixing breadcrumbs with the beaten egg instead of using pasta. A little very finely grated lemon peel can be added to the beaten egg if liked.

PASTA AND BEANS IN TOMATO SAUCE

(PASTA E FAGIOLI ALLA MARUZZARA)

2 cloves garlic
1 (225-g/8-oz) can tomatoes
olive oil
1 teaspoon crushed oregano
salt
2 (425-g/15-oz) cans cannellini beans
50 g/2 oz pasta per person

Start preparing the sauce just before cooking the pasta.

Peel the garlic and cut each clove into three or four pieces. Crush the tomatoes or blend them briefly in a liquidiser.

Coat the base of a large saucepan with olive oil and when it is hot, but not smoking, gently fry the garlic until golden. Add the tomatoes and the oregano, salt to taste, and simmer for about 10 minutes until the tomatoes are cooked. Add the beans and the juice from the cans and heat through, stirring all the time and adding a little water if necessary to keep the mixture very moist.

Drain the pasta a couple of minutes before it is perfectly cooked and add it to the soup. Mix thoroughly and allow to stand for approximately 5 minutes before serving, so that the heat of the bean sauce finishes cooking the pasta and the pasta absorbs the flavour of the sauce.

Pasta choice ditali, pasta mista, occhi di lupo, tubetti

COOK'S TIP

Some prefer this pasta dish thick, some as a thinner soup. The consistency can be adjusted by adding more or less water. This soup can obviously be made from dried cannellini beans which have been soaked overnight and boiled. In this case the sauce can be added to the beans and the pasta cooked in the bean soup. Canned beans are, however, much more convenient and the results are still very good.

MINESTRONE

Illustrated opposite

450 g/1 lb prepared mixed vegetables, for example, carrots, celery, leeks, courgettes, cabbage, spinach
2 ripe tomatoes
2 medium potatoes, peeled and diced
small bunch of parsley
50 g/2 oz rindless lean streaky bacon (unsliced)
1 clove garlic
olive oil
salt and pepper
100 g/4 oz canned cannellini beans
100 g/4 oz pasta
50 g/2 oz Parmesan cheese, grated

Minestrone is best made the day before serving though the pasta should be added just before eating.

Wash, trim and roughly chop the vegetables and parsley. Chop the bacon into small pieces. Peel the garlic clove and cut it into three or four pieces.

Coat the bottom of a large saucepan with olive oil and gently fry the garlic until golden and the bacon until crispy. Add the chopped and diced vegetables and enough water to cover them. Season to taste and simmer gently for about 40 minutes, until all the vegetables are cooked and have amalgamated into a thickish soup.

Add the canned beans and enough water to thin down the soup so that it will not become too thick while cooking the pasta.

Bring the soup to the boil and add the pasta. Cook according to the type of pasta used but testing it to see when it is ready.

Serve with the grated Parmesan.

Pasta choice ditalini, tubetti, occhi di lupo, conchigliette

Minestrone

COOK'S TIP

There are many ways of making minestrone. For people on a diet or those unable to eat fried foods, the vegetables may be boiled in water with one or two pieces of the rind of a hard cheese to give flavour instead of the fried bacon and garlic. Two tablespoons of olive oil should then be added to the finished soup, before the pasta is added. A pressure cooker is very useful for saving time.

USING UP LEFTOVERS

FRIED PASTA

(PASTA FRITTA)

olive oil
any leftover short pasta dressed with tomato or meat sauce

Heat the olive oil in a large frying pan and when it is hot, but not smoking, add the pasta. Stir occasionally and fry until the pasta becomes crisp.

Serve immediately with a little grated cheese if desired.

Pasta choice penne, rigatoni, sedani

COOK'S TIP
Leftover pasta will obviously be overcooked, but even the Italians are prepared to accept this when the dish is tasty. The pasta will have absorbed a large proportion of the sauce and is delicious when served hot and crunchy.

PIZZA MADE FROM PASTA

(PIZZA DI PASTA)

salami or cooked ham
egg
salt
leftover pasta dressed with tomato or meat sauce
grated Parmesan cheese
olive oil

Chop the salami or cooked ham into small pieces. Beat the egg and add salt to taste. Mix the pasta with the beaten egg, chopped cooked meat and grated cheese.

Cover the bottom of a large frying pan with olive oil and when it is hot, but not smoking, pour in the pasta mixture and press it down to form a flat surface. Allow to fry gently until the underside is golden and the egg has started to set. Using a plate the same size as the frying pan, turn the pizza over and fry until it is golden on the other side. Slide it out of the frying pan on to the plate and allow to cool.

Serve chilled and cut into slices.

Pasta choice any type except the very short pasta, but spaghetti is best.

COOK'S TIP
Prepare the pizza well in advance, as it should be served cold. Exact quantities of ingredients have not been given as it depends on the quantity of pasta which has been left over. The egg, however, should be sufficient to coat the pasta well and the other ingredients can be added as desired.

Note: this pizza is often made in Italy to take to the beach or on a picnic. It can also be served at a cold buffet party.

Pasta Salad

(Insalata di Pasta)

fresh tomatoes
green olives
pickled vegetables
tuna
undressed leftover pasta
olive oil
salt and freshly ground black pepper

Prepare the salad well in advance of serving so that it is well chilled.

Cut the tomatoes into very small pieces, removing the seeds. Stone the olives and cut them into thin slices. Roughly chop the pickled vegetables.

Drain the juice from the tuna and break the tuna into small pieces. Mix the pasta with the prepared ingredients, adding olive oil and salt and freshly ground black pepper to taste. Allow to stand in the fridge for approximately 2 hours before serving.

Pasta choice tubetti or any other very short pasta.

Cook's Tip

Chopped ham or luncheon meat, or small pieces of chicken breast or turkey can be used instead of tuna fish. A variety of different fresh vegetables can also be added instead of the pickles if you prefer.

The exact quantity of ingredients has not been given as it depends on how much pasta is left over and on personal taste.

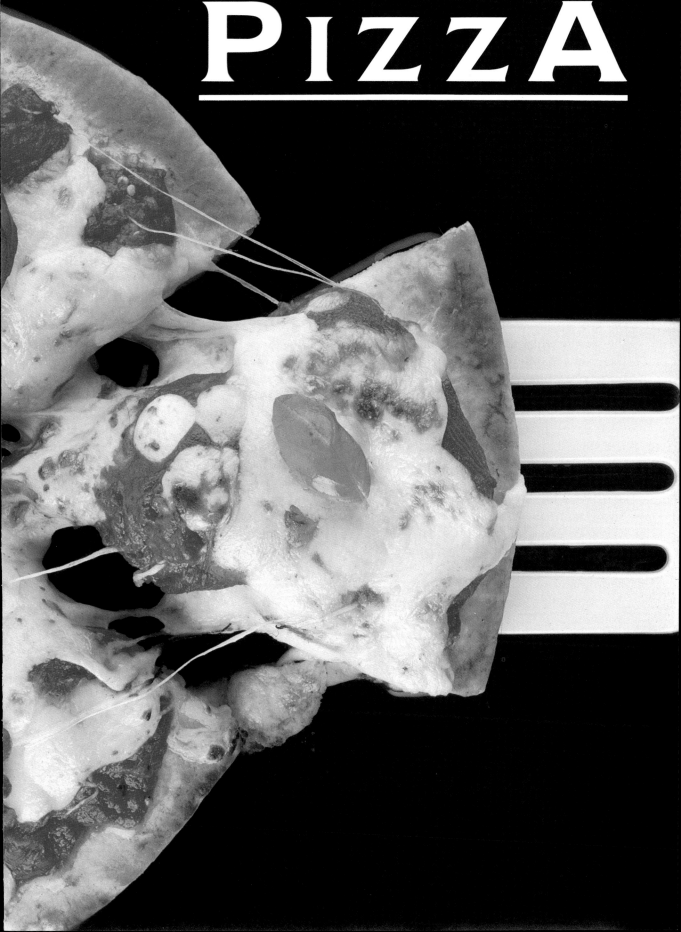

PIZZA

HISTORICAL BACKGROUND

Although he did not realise it, Stone Age man was probably the inventor of the pizza. He mixed together ground wheat and water to form a type of dough, and cooked it in discs on or between flat stones which had been heated up in the fire. Primitive man continued to bake 'bread' in this way until the time of the ancient Egyptians, who invented the conical-shaped stone oven which was similar to the modern pizza oven of today. They used to bake their bread discs by sticking them to the hot outside walls of the oven, turning them over when they fell off and cooking them on the other side. The Egyptians left no record of having made pizzas, but there are references to a type of pizza made by the Greeks and Romans, which they topped with olives, honey or various other herbs and spices.

The name 'pizza' probably originated in Naples around 1000 A.D., where flat discs of a bread-like substance were first called 'picea' and then 'piza'.

Pizzas, as we know them today, can be traced back to the 1700s. They appeared long after the introduction into Europe of the tomato, which originated in Peru. Previously this 'strange fruit' was used as an ornamental plant. It was later discovered that it could be put to better use. At first, pizzas were made and sold by the roadside on stalls and it was not until the early 1800s that the first Pizzeria appeared in Naples, where people could sit down at a table and enjoy their favourite pizza accompanied by a glass of local wine.

Though well known, it is worth telling the famous story about the most renowned pizza – Pizza Margherita. In the late 1800s Queen Margherita was resident, as she was every summer, with her family at their lodge in Capodimonte Park in Naples.

Having heard so much talk about an innovation called pizza, she summoned the most famous Neapolitan pizzaiuolo (pizza-maker), Don Raffaele Esposito, to court and demanded to taste this new dish. The pizzaiuolo was so proud and honoured to show off his art that, apart from preparing the usual toppings which he served nightly in his pizzeria, he invented a special one, topped with mozzarella cheese, for his royal guest. (Some say that it was Don Raffaele's wife's idea!) Queen Margherita was so taken with the special pizza that Don Raffaele named the pizza 'Margherita' to commemorate the occasion. It continues to be one of the most popular pizzas in Italy today.

The majority of pizzerias in Italy are still family businesses, but chains of pizzerias have sprung up all over the western world. Naples has, however, remained the home of the pizza and even in Italy pizzas made outside this city tend to have a different flavour.

The art of pizza making depends not only on the ingredients and the handling of the dough but also on the type of oven used. A real pizza should be baked in a wood-fuelled oven next to the charcoal embers. This is what gives the pizza its typical flavour. It is a great shame that present legislation in some countries does not allow the use of open-fire ovens in restaurants. A pizza cooked in an electric oven is a poor substitute.

HOW TO MAKE A PIZZA

There are many different ways of making pizza dough. Some add oil, some add an egg, some make a dough first with part of the flour mixed with the yeast, allow it to rise and then knead it into the rest of the flour and water. (This is the method used by Italian bakers to make bread.) After experimenting with these many different methods I have found that there is, in fact, not that much difference in the finished product provided that you follow a few simple rules:

1 Always use strong plain flour.
2 Make sure that the water used is tepid and not hot.
3 If you are using dried yeast, use part of the quantity of water given in the pizza recipe to reconstitute it. (The packet can be misleading.)
4 The dough really must be kneaded for about 10 minutes – there is no short cut!
5 The dough must be allowed to rise covered, and away from draughts, until it has doubled in size.
6 If the pizza dough rises more quickly than you expected, you can knock it back and leave it to rise for a little longer.
7 Always preheat the oven for at least 20 minutes before baking the pizza to make sure that it has reached the required temperature.
8 Use lard, instead of oil, for greasing the baking tray as it will be easier to press the pizza into shape. (It is stickier!)
9 Use a thin baking tray for baking the pizza as it will cook through better.
10 When starting to shape the pizza, you must really slap it down hard on to the floured table three or four times to eliminate any excess gases which may have formed during the leavening. (This is marvellous for getting rid of any pent up frustrations or anger, too!)
11 After shaping the pizza leave it to rest on the baking tray for approximately 15–20 minutes before adding the topping. The resulting pizza will be much lighter.
12 When adding the topping be careful not to spread it over the border. Never overload the pizza with topping or the dough underneath will not cook sufficiently and will be soggy.
13 Bake the pizza until it has risen well, the topping is cooked and the borders are golden.
14 Serve the pizza immediately. Cold or reheated pizzas are never the same.

Watching a real pizza-maker prepare his pizzas is a sight worth seeing. He tosses them in the air and slaps them down on the marble table with great gusto. I do not expect that any of us will ever match the performance of a true Neapolitan pizzaiuolo, but making pizzas is really easier than it would seem, once you have acquired the knack, and there are so many toppings to choose from, try out and invent, that it is well worth the effort. Pizzas certainly add variation and colour to your daily menus.

PIZZA SHAPES

Round Pizzas Turn the dough out on to the floured working surface and knead it two or three times. Start flattening and gently pulling the ball of dough out into a circle, working from the centre outwards, taking care not to tear the pizza. Pick it up, and holding it vertically and working very quickly, turn it in an anti-clockwise direction between the thumb and forefinger of both hands as if you were turning a plate. Slap the pizza down onto the working surface vigorously and repeat this process two or three times until the circle is almost the required size.

Place the circle of dough on a greased baking tray and gently push it outwards from the centre until you reach the size needed. Form a thin border around the edges.

Leave the pizza to rise for approximately 15–20 minutes before adding the topping.

Rectangular Pizzas (*Pizza a taglio*) Turn the dough out on to the floured working surface and knead it two or three times. Start flattening and

continued on page 124

MAKING PIZZA

1   Sift the flour and salt into a bowl. Make a well in the centre of the flour and pour in the frothy yeast.

2   Beat the dough hard with your hand.

3   Knead the dough well on a lightly floured work surface.

4   Shape the dough into a round with the heel of the hand.

5   For Mushroom and Mozzarella Topping (page 137), spoon tomatoes on to the pizza, used whole here instead of chopped.

6   Sprinkle over the diced mozzarella and arrange the mushrooms on top of the cheese. The cooked pizza is shown opposite.

gently pulling it out into a rectangle, lifting it up and slapping it down on to the table vigorously to eliminate the excess gases. Use a floured rolling pin to help you reach the required size. Lift the rectangle of dough on to the greased baking tray and push it, using your fingers, to the sides and into the corners of the tin. Form a thin border around the edges. Leave the pizza to rise for about 15–20 minutes before adding the topping.

Thickness There are two schools of pizza-making: the Neapolitan and the Roman. The Neapolitans make slightly thicker pizzas (3–5 mm/$\frac{1}{8}$–$\frac{1}{4}$ in) with a thicker and deeper border in order to contain a richer topping. The Romans make a flatter pizza, about 3-mm/$\frac{1}{8}$-in thick, which is more biscuit-like. The Roman pizza tends to be drier than the Neapolitan one as the smaller quantity of topping is more easily absorbed by the dough in the baking.

The given quantities of topping are for Roman-style pizzas and all cover one large, two medium, or four small pizzas. (See note on sizes under the Basic pizza dough recipe which follows.)

Basic Pizza Dough

25 g/1 oz fresh yeast
300 ml/$\frac{1}{2}$ pint tepid water
400 g/14 oz strong plain flour plus extra for working the dough
1 teaspoon salt

Blend the yeast with part of the tepid water. Sieve the flour and salt into a large mixing bowl. Make a well in the centre and pour in the yeast mixture and the remaining tepid water. Using your hand, and with a circular movement, gradually work the flour into the liquid moving from the centre of the well outwards to form a sticky, elastic dough.

Turn the dough out on to a floured working surface and knead it well, adding more flour if necessary, until it stops sticking to your knuckles and the working surface. Knead it well for approximately 10 minutes until it becomes smooth and elastic.

At this stage, if you are making more than one pizza, divide the dough into the required number of pieces and knead each one into a ball. Sprinkle the bottom of the mixing bowl with flour and leave the dough to rise, covering the bowl with a cloth, for approximately 1 hour. The time required will depend on the warmth of the kitchen. The dough is ready when it has doubled in size.

The dough can be shaped into two large round pizzas of approximately 30 cm/12 in. in diameter, one large rectangular pizza, or four individual pizzas of approximately 20 cm/8 in. in diameter. Pizza tins are available in most well-stocked hardware stores. These will help you to shape the pizza better.

Potato Dough

1 (150-g/5-oz) potato
400 g/14 oz strong plain flour
1 teaspoon salt
25 g/1 oz fresh yeast
350 ml/12 fl oz tepid water

Scrub the potato and boil it in its jacket for approximately 30–40 minutes, until well cooked. Peel and mash the potato, passing it through a sieve. Add the potato to the flour and salt when adding the yeast and water. Continue working the dough as for the basic pizza dough.

Like basic pizza dough this quantity will make one large, two medium or four small pizzas.

Cook's Tip
The addition of the potato makes a softer, lighter pizza.

OIL AND GARLIC TOPPING

(AGLIO E OLIO)

6 cloves garlic
1 quantity Basic Pizza Dough (page 124)
3 tablespoons olive oil
salt
1 teaspoon crushed oregano

Peel and chop the garlic cloves into small pieces and sprinkle them over the pizza. Pour the oil over the top and sprinkle with salt and dried oregano.

Bake at the top of a very hot oven (240 C, 475 F, gas 9) for approximately 15–20 minutes, until the pizza has risen and turned golden brown.

COOK'S TIP

Freshly ground black pepper can be substituted for the oregano if preferred. Do not make any engagements for one or two days after eating this!

VEGETABLE TOPPINGS

OLIVE OIL AND SEA SALT TOPPING

(PIZZA BIANCA)

1 quantity Basic Pizza Dough (page 124)
olive oil
freshly ground sea salt

Brush the surface of the pizza abundantly with the olive oil. Sprinkle with freshly ground sea salt.

Bake at the top of a very hot oven (240 C, 475 F, gas 9) for 15–20 minutes, until the pizza has risen and become crisp and golden in colour.

COOK'S TIP

This pizza is usually served in the place of bread or can be eaten as a snack.

OIL AND GARLIC TOPPING (UNCOOKED)

1 quantity Basic Pizza Dough (page 124)
1–4 cloves garlic
olive oil
salt

Bake the pizza without any topping. When it is ready, rub the surface with the clove of garlic, brush it with olive oil and sprinkle with salt. Serve immediately while still hot.

COOK'S TIP
This pizza can be served in the place of bread at a meal.

POTATO TOPPING

(CON PATATE)

Illustrated opposite

4 medium potatoes
1 quantity Basic Pizza Dough (page 124)
olive oil
salt
dried or fresh rosemary

Peel the potatoes and cut them into very thin slices of no more than 3 mm/$\frac{1}{8}$ in thick. Arrange these slices on the top of the pizza, overlapping them slightly. Brush the potatoes well with olive oil, sprinkle with salt and rosemary.

Bake at the top of a very hot oven (240 C, 475 F, gas 9) for approximately 20–25 minutes, until the pizza has risen and the potatoes are cooked.

COOK'S TIP
If the potatoes do not brown sufficiently in the oven you can always put the pizza under the grill for a few minutes.

Note: this is one of the toppings served in the pizza shops which sell pizza 'al metro' – by the yard!

Top: *Pizza with Potato Topping*
Bottom: *Pizza with Peppers (2) (page 131)*

TOMATO AND OREGANO TOPPING

(POMODORO E ORIGANO)

1 (227-g/8-oz) can tomatoes
2 cloves garlic
1 quantity Basic Pizza Dough (page 124)
1 teaspoon crushed oregano
salt
2 tablespoons olive oil

Crush the tomatoes or blend them briefly in a liquidiser. Peel and finely chop the garlic cloves. Spread the surface of the pizza with the tomatoes and sprinkle with chopped garlic, crushed oregano and salt. Pour the oil over the pizza.

Bake at the top of a very hot oven (240 C, 475 F, gas 9) for about 15–20 minutes, until the pizza has risen and the borders are golden brown.

ONION TOPPING

(CON CIPOLLE)

2 large onions
1 quantity Basic Pizza Dough (page 124)
olive oil
salt and pepper

Cut the onions into very thin rings of no more than 3 mm/$\frac{1}{8}$ in thick. Arrange the rings on top of the pizza, brush them with olive oil and sprinkle them with salt and pepper.

Bake at the top of a very hot oven (240 C, 475 F, gas 9) for approximately 20–25 minutes, until the pizza has risen and the onions are soft and beginning to brown.

COOK'S TIP

The onions can be browned under the grill if they are cooked sufficiently with the pizza.

COURGETTE TOPPING

(CON ZUCCHINE)

4 medium courgettes
1 large onion
1 quantity Basic Pizza Dough (page 124)
salt and pepper
2 tablespoons olive oil

Wash, dry and cut the courgettes into very thin rings of approximately 1.5 mm/$\frac{1}{16}$in. Finely chop the onion. Sprinkle the pizza with the chopped onion and arrange the courgette rings on top. Sprinkle with salt and pepper and pour the oil over the pizza.

Bake at the top of a very hot oven (240 C, 475 F, gas 9) for approximately 20 minutes until the pizza is cooked and the courgettes are soft.

COOK'S TIP

Grated Parmesan cheese can be added to the pizza before baking, if desired.

PIZZA WITH PEPPERS (1)

(CON PEPERONI)

Illustrated on page 127

2 large red or yellow peppers
1 medium onion
1 quantity Basic Pizza Dough (page 124)
2 tablespoons olive oil
salt

Wash the peppers and put them to roast in the oven for approximately 30–40 minutes, turning them occasionally, until the skins have started to come away.

Peel the peppers and discard the seeds. Break them with your fingers into long, thin strips. Finely chop the onion. Brush the pizza with olive oil, sprinkle with the chopped onion and arrange the strips of peppers on top. Sprinkle with salt and pour the rest of the olive oil over the pizza.

Bake at the top of a very hot oven (240 C, 475 F, gas 9) for approximately 20 minutes, until the pizza has risen and the border is golden.

COOK'S TIP

If you prefer green peppers, then add a little tomato to make a pleasing colour combination.

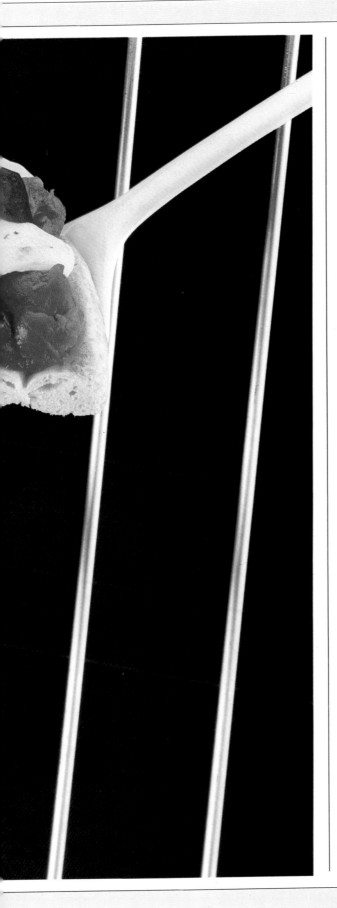

PIZZA WITH PEPPERS (2)

2 cloves garlic
2 large red peppers
1 quantity Basic Pizza Dough (page 124)
salt
1 teaspoon crushed oregano
2 tablespoons olive oil

Peel and finely chop the garlic. Wash, dry and cut the peppers into very thin rings of approximately 3 mm/$\frac{1}{8}$ in, discarding the seeds. Arrange the slices of peppers on top of the pizza, sprinkle with the chopped garlic, salt and oregano and pour the oil over the top.

Bake at the top of a very hot oven (240 C, 475 F, gas 9) for approximately 20–25 minutes, until the pizza has risen and the peppers are cooked.

COOK'S TIP

Black olives and capers can be added and the oregano omitted if preferred. If using oregano, be careful not to add too much as it can give the pizza a bitter flavour.

Top: *Pizza with Aubergine Topping (page 134)*
Bottom: *Pizza with Artichoke Topping (page 132)*

ARTICHOKE TOPPING

(AI CARCIOFI)

Illustrated on page 130

**4 globe artichokes
juice of $\frac{1}{2}$ lemon
225 g/8 oz Emmental cheese
1 quantity Basic Pizza Dough (page 124)
salt and pepper
2 tablespoons olive oil**

Prepare the artichokes by pulling off the tough outside leaves until those underneath are whitish. Cut off the top third of the artichokes to eliminate the tips of the leaves. Peel the stalk, leaving the tender core. Rub the prepared artichokes with lemon juice and leave them in cold water and lemon juice for approximately 15 minutes.

Drain the artichokes well and cut them lengthways into very thin wedges of approximately 3 mm/$\frac{1}{8}$ in, and the stalks into very thin strips. Grate the cheese. Arrange the artichokes on top of the pizza, sprinkle with salt, pepper and grated cheese. Pour the oil over the top.

Bake at the top of a very hot oven (240 C, 475 F, gas 9) for approximately 25–30 minutes, until the pizza has risen, the artichokes are cooked and the cheese is golden brown.

COOK'S TIP
The use of lemon when preparing the artichokes removes their bitter taste, and prevents them from turning brown. Cheese slices can be used instead of the grated Emmental if preferred.

MUSHROOM TOPPING

(AI FUNGHI)

**1 (227-g/8-oz) can tomatoes
1 clove garlic
8 large mushrooms
1 quantity Basic Pizza Dough (page 124)
salt and freshly ground black pepper
2 tablespoons olive oil**

Crush the tomatoes or blend them briefly in a liquidiser. Peel and crush the clove of garlic and mix it with the tomatoes. Wash, dry and cut the mushrooms into very thin slices.

Spread the tomatoes over the pizza and arrange the sliced mushrooms on top. Sprinkle with salt and plenty of freshly ground black pepper and pour the oil over the top.

Bake at the top of a very hot oven (240 C, 475 F, gas 9) for approximately 20–25 minutes, until the pizza has risen and the topping is cooked.

COOK'S TIP
Field mushrooms are preferable to button mushrooms as they have more flavour.

CANNELLINI BEAN TOPPING

(CON FAGIOLI)

**1 small onion, or 2 spring onions, or small
bunch of chives
2 sticks celery
2 (425-g/15-oz) cans cannellini beans
salt and freshly ground black pepper
1 quantity Basic Pizza Dough (page 124)
1 tablespoon chopped parsley
2 tablespoons olive oil**

Finely chop the onion and celery. Heat the beans in a saucepan until just warmed through, add the onion, celery and salt and freshly ground black pepper to taste.

Bake the pizza without the topping at the top of a very hot oven (240 C, 475 F, gas 9) for about 15 minutes, until well risen and golden.

Remove from the oven and pour the bean mixture on top of the pizza. Sprinkle with chopped parsley and pour the oil over the top.

FRESH TOMATO TOPPING

(CON POMODORI FRESCHI)

**8 medium ripe tomatoes
1 quantity Basic Pizza Dough (page 124)
salt and pepper
25 g/1 oz butter**

Wash, dry and slice the tomatoes into very thin rings of approximately 3 mm/$\frac{1}{8}$ in. Arrange the slices of tomato on top of the pizza, sprinkle with salt and pepper and cover with flakes of butter.

Bake at the top of a very hot oven (240 C, 475 F, gas 9) for approximately 15–20 minutes, until the pizza is well risen and the tomatoes are cooked.

COOK'S TIP
Grated cheese or cheese slices can be added if wished. This must be the Italian version of tomatoes on toast!

AUBERGINE TOPPING

(ALLE MELANZANE)

Illustrated on page 130

**2 medium aubergines
coarse sea salt
olive oil
1 (227-g/8-oz) can tomatoes
2 cloves garlic
225 g/8 oz mozzarella cheese
1 quantity Basic Pizza Dough (page 124)**

Wash, dry and cut the aubergines into cubes of approximately 1.5 cm/¾ in. Do not peel them. Put the cubes in a colander with layers of coarse sea salt, place a weight on top and leave them for approximately 30 minutes to allow the salt to draw the bitterness out of the aubergines. Rinse off all the salt and squeeze the aubergines well to remove as much liquid as possible.

Fry the cubes in olive oil and drain them on kitchen paper. Crush the tomatoes, or blend them briefly in a liquidiser. Peel and finely chop the garlic. Roughly grate the mozzarella cheese. Spread the tomatoes on the pizza, sprinkle with chopped garlic. Cover the pizza with the aubergine cubes and top with the grated mozzarella cheese. Pour 2 tablespoons olive oil over the top.

Bake at the top of a very hot oven (240 C, 475 F, gas 9) for approximately 20–25 minutes, until the pizza has risen well and the mozzarella has melted and started to turn golden.

COOK'S TIP
Do not add any salt to the pizza topping as the aubergines remain slightly salty after being rinsed and squeezed out.

SAILOR'S-STYLE TOPPING

(ALLA MARINARA)

**1 generous tablespoon capers
1 (227-g/8-oz) can tomatoes
100 g/4 oz black olives
1 quantity Basic Pizza Dough (page 124)
salt and freshly ground black pepper
2 tablespoons olive oil**

Rinse and dry the capers if they have been salted. Crush the tomatoes or blend them briefly in a liquidiser. Stone the olives and cut each one into three or four pieces.

Spread the tomatoes over the pizza and add the capers and olives. Sprinkle with salt and plenty of freshly ground black pepper, then pour the oil over the top.

Bake at the top of a very hot oven (240 C, 475 F, gas 9) for 20–25 minutes, until the pizza has risen well and the border is golden.

COOK'S TIP
Some people add one or two boned anchovy fillets to this topping.

Pizza Margherita (page 136)

CHEESE TOPPINGS

PIZZA MARGHERITA

Illustrated on page 135

**1 (400-g/14-oz) can tomatoes
225 g/8 oz mozzarella cheese
8–10 fresh basil leaves
1 quantity Basic Pizza Dough (page 124)
salt
2 tablespoons grated Parmesan cheese
2 tablespoons olive oil**

Crush or roughly chop the tomatoes. Roughly chop the mozzarella cheese into small pieces. Wash and dry the basil leaves.

Spoon the tomatoes over the pizza and sprinkle them with salt. Sprinkle the pieces of mozzarella cheese over the pizza, distributing them evenly. Break the basil leaves into small pieces between your fingers and distribute them evenly over the top. (For our illustration small basil leaves were used whole.) Sprinkle the Parmesan over the pizza, then pour on the oil.

Bake at the top of a very hot oven (240 C, 475 F, gas 9) for approximately 20–25 minutes, until the pizza is well risen and the cheese has melted and started to turn golden.

COOK'S TIP
This is probably the most famous pizza topping both in Italy and abroad. (See notes on the history of the pizza.)

THREE CHEESES TOPPING

(AI TRE FORMAGGI)

**100 g/4 oz mozzarella cheese
100 g/4 oz Emmental or Gruyère cheese
100 g/4 oz Parmesan cheese, grated
1 quantity Basic Pizza Dough (page 124)
2 tablespoons olive oil**

Roughly grate the mozzarella and Swiss cheese and mix them with the grated Parmesan.

Sprinkle the cheeses over the pizza and pour the oil on the top.

Bake at the top of a very hot oven (240 C, 475 F, gas 9) for approximately 15–20 minutes, until the pizza has risen well and the cheeses have melted and are golden brown.

COOK'S TIP
The number of cheeses used can be varied from two to five and different types may be used.

PARMESAN AND LARD TOPPING

(SUGNA E PARMIGIANO)

1 quantity Basic Pizza Dough (page 124)
50 g/2 oz lard
2 generous tablespoons grated Parmesan cheese
1 tablespoon chopped parsley
salt and freshly ground black pepper

Cover the pizza with flakes of lard and sprinkle with grated Parmesan cheese, chopped parsley, salt and freshly ground black pepper.

Bake at the top of a very hot oven (240 C, 475 F, gas 9) for approximately 20 minutes, until the pizza has risen and the cheese has turned golden.

COOK'S TIP
Fresh basil can be used instead of parsley if preferred.

MUSHROOM AND MOZZARELLA TOPPING

(CON FUNGHI E MOZZARELLA)

1 (400-g/14-oz) can tomatoes
225 g/8 oz mozzarella cheese
100 g/4 oz medium mushrooms
1 quantity Basic Pizza Dough (page 124)
salt
2 tablespoons olive oil
freshly ground black pepper (optional)

Crush or roughly chop the tomatoes. Roughly chop or grate the mozzarella cheese into small pieces. Wash, peel and thinly slice the mushrooms.

Spread the tomatoes over the pizza and sprinkle them with salt. Sprinkle the mozzarella cheese evenly over the pizza. Arrange the sliced mushrooms on the top, sprinkle with salt and pour the oil over the pizza.

Bake at the top of a very hot oven (240 C, 475 F, gas 9) for approximately 20 minutes, until the pizza has risen well and the cheese has turned golden.

CHEESE AND ONION TOPPING

(CIPOLLE E FORMAGGIO)

2 large onions
150 g/5 oz Gruyère or Emmental cheese
1 quantity Basic Pizza Dough (page 124)
salt
2 tablespoons olive oil

Cut the onions into very thin rings not more than 3 mm/$\frac{1}{8}$ in thick. Grate the cheese. Arrange the onion rings on top of the pizza and sprinkle them with salt. Cover the onions with the grated cheese and pour the oil over the pizza.

Bake at the top of a very hot oven (240 C, 475 F, gas 9) for approximately 20–25 minutes, until the pizza has risen and the cheese is golden brown.

COOK'S TIP
The Swiss cheese can be substituted by another of your choice, such as Cheddar.

APPLE AND GORGONZOLA TOPPING

(MELA E GORGONZOLA)

2 large cooking apples
350 g/12 oz Gorgonzola cheese
1 quantity Basic Pizza Dough (page 124)
2 tablespoons olive oil

Peel, core and cut the apples into very small cubes of approximately 1 cm/$\frac{1}{2}$ in, leaving a few thin slices of apple for decorating the pizza. Mix the apple with the Gorgonzola cheese and spread the mixture on top of the pizza.

Decorate with the slices of apple and pour the oil over the top.

Bake the pizza at the top of a very hot oven (240 C, 475 F, gas 9) for about 20 minutes, until the pizza has risen well and the topping has started to turn golden.

COOK'S TIP
The creamy variety of Gorgonzola is best for this topping as it will mix better with the apple and melt when cooked.

MEAT TOPPINGS

BACON AND EGG TOPPING

(UOVA E PANCETTA)

Illustrated opposite

1 quantity Basic Pizza Dough (page 124)
1 (227-g/8-oz) can tomatoes
salt and pepper
8 rindless rashers lean streaky bacon
2 tablespoons olive oil
4 fresh eggs

Make four individual pizzas with the dough.

Crush the tomatoes or blend them briefly in a liquidiser and spread them over the pizzas, taking care not to cover the borders. Sprinkle them with salt and pepper. Arrange the rashers of bacon around the inside of the borders and pour the oil over the top.

Bake the pizzas at the top of a very hot oven (240 C, 475 F, gas 9) for approximately 15 minutes. Take the pizzas out of the oven and break an egg on to the middle of each one. Put them back in the oven until the whites of the eggs have set but the yolks are still liquid, which takes about another 10 minutes.

COOK'S TIP

The eggs must be very fresh so that they will stay in the centre of the pizza. (Fresh eggs are much less liquid than those which have been around for a few days!)

Pizza with Bacon and Egg Topping

GAMMON AND PINEAPPLE TOPPING

(GAMMON E ANANAS)

225 g/8 oz gammon
1 (227-g/8-oz) can pineapple rings, or
225 g/8 oz fresh pineapple, chopped
1 quantity Basic Pizza Dough (page 124)
2 tablespoons olive oil

Trim the fat off the gammon and cut the meat into small cubes of approximately 1 cm/½ in. Drain the juice off the pineapple, crush the fruit and mix it with the chopped gammon.

Cover the pizza with the mixture and pour the oil over the top.

Bake at the top of a very hot oven (240 C, 475 F, gas 9) for approximately 20 minutes, until the pizza has risen well and the gammon is cooked.

Parma Ham and Mozzarella Topping

(Prosciutto e Mozzarella)

150 g/5 oz Parma ham
1 quantity Basic Pizza Dough (page 124)
225 g/8 oz mozzarella cheese
2 tablespoons olive oil

Cut the Parma ham into matchstick-sized strips and cover the pizza with them. Grate the mozzarella cheese and sprinkle it over the ham. Pour the oil over the top.

Bake at the top of a very hot oven (240 c, 475 f, gas 9) for approximately 20 minutes.

Cook's Tip

Do not cut the fat off the ham as this helps to keep it moist during the cooking.

Spicy Sausage Topping (1)

(Con Salsicce)

1 small onion
6 spicy Italian sausages
1 tablespoon olive oil
$\frac{1}{2}$ glass dry white wine
1 quantity Basic Pizza Dough (page 124)

Finely chop the onion. Skin the sausages and crumble the meat between your fingers to separate it.

Coat the bottom of a frying pan with the olive oil and gently fry the chopped onion until it is transparent. Add the sausage meat and fry gently, stirring all the time to separate the pieces of meat. Add the wine and allow it to evaporate.

Spread the mixture over the pizza.

Bake at the top of a very hot oven (240 c, 475 f, gas 9) for approximately 20 minutes, until the pizza has risen well.

Cook's Tip

English pork sausages can be used if you add a little freshly ground black pepper.

SPICY SAUSAGE TOPPING (2)

6 spicy Italian sausages
1 (227-g/8-oz) can tomatoes
1 quantity Basic Pizza Dough (page 124)
salt
1 tablespoon olive oil

Skin the sausages and break the meat between your fingers. Crush the tomatoes or blend them briefly in a liquidiser and spread them over the pizza. Sprinkle with a little salt and cover the pizza with the crumbled sausage meat. Pour the oil over the top.

Bake at the top of a very hot oven (240 C, 475 F, gas 9) for approximately 25 minutes, until the pizza has risen well and the sausages are cooked.

COOK'S TIP
Italian sausages already contain a lot of fat so less olive oil is needed. If you are using English sausages you may need to add a little more oil.

FOUR SEASONS
(QUATTRO STAGIONI)

1 quantity Basic Pizza Dough (page 124)
4 different types of pizza toppings

Before shaping the pizzas, break off a small piece of pizza dough. Roll this into thin strips and use these to divide each pizza into four parts as you would a jam tart.

Put the four different toppings on the top of each pizza.

Bake at the top of a very hot oven (240 C, 475 F, gas 9) for approximately 20–25 minutes, until the pizzas have risen and the toppings are cooked.

COOK'S TIP
The classical four seasons pizza is made up of: ham and mozzarella, margherita, marinara and mushrooms.

FISH AND SEAFOOD TOPPINGS

TUNA TOPPING

(AL TONNO)

Illustrated opposite

**1 (400-g/14-oz) can tomatoes
6 black olives
1 small onion
olive oil
salt and freshly ground black pepper
1 (198-g/7-oz) can tuna, drained and flaked
1 quantity Basic Pizza Dough (page 124)**

Crush or roughly chop the tomatoes. Stone the olives and cut each one into three or four pieces. Finely chop the onion.

Coat the bottom of a large frying pan with olive oil and gently fry the onion until it is transparent. Add the tomatoes and simmer gently, adding salt to taste, until the sauce becomes denser. Add the tuna and continue to cook for another five minutes. Allow the sauce to cool.

Spread the sauce over the pizza, sprinkle generously with freshly ground black pepper and decorate with the olives. Add a little olive oil.

Bake at the top of a very hot oven (240 C, 475 F, gas 9) for approximately 20 minutes, until the pizza is well risen and the border is golden brown.

COOK'S TIP
One or two crushed anchovy fillets may be added to the sauce to give it a stronger flavour.

PIZZA WITH TUNA FISH SALAD

(ALL' INSALATA DI TONNO)

**8 medium tomatoes
1 stick celery
2 spring onions
1 (198-g/7-oz) can tuna, drained and flaked
1 quantity Basic Pizza Dough (page 124)
salt and freshly ground black pepper
2 tablespoons olive oil**

Peel and deseed the tomatoes. Roughly chop the pulp. Thinly slice the celery and the onions and mix them with the tomato and the tuna.

Leave the mixture to cool in the refrigerator while the pizza is baking.

Bake the pizza without the topping at the top of a very hot oven (240 C, 475 F, gas 9) for about 15 minutes, until it is well risen and the border is golden.

Remove the pizza from the oven, season the tomato mixture with salt and freshly ground black pepper and arrange it on top of the pizza. Pour the olive oil over the top and serve immediately.

COOK'S TIP
Do not season the tomatoes until you are ready to serve them or they will become very watery. Stoned, green olives can be added to the salad if desired. The combination of the hot pizza and the cool salad is very pleasant, especially on a hot summer's day.

Pizza with Tuna Topping

CAVIAR TOPPING

(CON CAVIALE)

1 medium onion
1 quantity Basic Pizza Dough (page 124)
1 small jar of caviar
1 teaspoon roughly chopped parsley
2 tablespoons olive oil

Finely chop the onion and spread it over the pizza. Sprinkle the caviar over the pizza, add the chopped parsley and pour the oil over the top.

Bake at the top of a very hot oven (240 C, 475 F, gas 9) for approximately 15–20 minutes until the pizza has risen well and the borders are golden.

COOK'S TIP

It is not necessary to use best Russian caviar for this dish, or it will be too expensive to even contemplate!

PRAWN TOPPING

(CON GAMBERI)

1 (400-g/14-oz) can tomatoes
2 cloves garlic
olive oil
1 small chilli
350 g/12 oz frozen peeled prawns, thawed
salt
1 quantity Basic Pizza Dough (page 124)
1 teaspoon chopped parsley

Crush the tomatoes or blend them briefly in a liquidiser. Peel the garlic and cut each clove into three or four pieces.

Coat the bottom of a frying pan with olive oil and when it is hot, but not smoking, add the garlic and the chilli. Fry gently until the garlic is golden, rubbing the chilli against the bottom of the pan to release its flavour. Add the tomatoes and simmer gently, adding the prawns and salt to taste after about 10 minutes. Cook for a further 5 minutes to allow the prawns to heat through.

Bake the pizza without the topping for about 15 minutes. When it is well risen and golden, remove it from the oven and pour the prawns on the top.

Garnish with the chopped parsley and serve immediately.

ANCHOVY, CAPERS AND OLIVE TOPPING

(CON ALICI, CAPPERI E OLIVE)

I (227-g/8-oz) can tomatoes
10 black olives
I tablespoon capers
8 anchovy fillets
I quantity Basic Pizza Dough (page 124)
2 tablespoons olive oil

Crush the tomatoes or blend them briefly in a liquidiser. Stone the olives and cut each one into three or four pieces. Rinse and dry the capers if they have been preserved in salt.

Break the anchovy fillets into small pieces. Spread the tomatoes over the pizza and add the anchovy fillets, the capers and the olives. Pour the oil over the top.

Bake at the top of a very hot oven (240 C, 475 F, gas 9) for approximately 20 minutes, until the pizza has risen well and the borders are golden.

COOK'S TIP

This is a very strong-flavoured pizza and is not to everyone's taste.

ROMAN-STYLE PIZZA

(ALLA ROMANA)

Illustrated on pages 146 and 147

I (227-g/8-oz) can tomatoes
225 g/8 oz mozzarella cheese
6 anchovy fillets
I quantity Basic Pizza Dough (page 124)
salt
2 tablespoons olive oil

Crush the tomatoes or blend them briefly in a liquidiser. Roughly grate the mozzarella cheese. Break the anchovy fillets into small pieces.

Spread the tomato over the pizza and sprinkle it with a little salt and the grated mozzarella. Arrange the pieces of anchovy fillet on the top and pour the oil over the pizza.

Bake at the top of a very hot oven (240 C, 475 F, gas 9) for approximately 20 minutes, until the pizza has risen well and the mozzarella has melted. The border should be golden brown.

Note: this pizza is called *alla Romana* in Naples and *alla Napoletana* in Rome.

FISHERMAN'S TOPPING

(ALLA PESCATORA)

Illustrated opposite

225 g/8 oz fresh mussels (in their shells)
1 (400-g/14-oz) can tomatoes
2 cloves garlic
olive oil
100 g/4 oz squid, cleaned and cut into pieces
salt and freshly ground black pepper
225 g/8 oz cleaned, shelled clams
100 g/4 oz cleaned fresh prawns
1 quantity Basic Pizza Dough (page 124)
small bunch of parsley, chopped

Scrub the mussels well to remove any seaweed or other impurities on the shells and pull out the byssus from each mussel. (The tuft of silky filament by which the mussels attach themselves to the rocks.) Put the mussels in a large pan over the heat, cover, and toss them occasionally to allow all the mussels to open. Throw away any which have not opened. (See note on mussels on page 88). Strain and reserve the resulting liquid.

Crush the tomatoes or blend them briefly in a liquidiser. Peel and cut each clove of garlic into three or four pieces.

Cover the bottom of the frying pan with olive oil and when the oil is hot, but not smoking, add the garlic and fry it gently until golden. Add the squid which have been cut into small pieces and allow them to fry gently for 5 minutes, then remove with a slotted spoon. Add the tomatoes and a tablespoon of the juice from the mussels. Salt to taste and simmer gently for about 30 minutes, adding the clams and the prawns 10 minutes before the end. Add the mussels in their shells and squid and allow to heat through.

Bake the pizza without the topping at the top of a very hot oven (240 C, 475 F, gas 9) for about 15 minutes, until it is well risen and the border is golden brown.

Remove from the oven and arrange the seafood on the top. Sprinkle generously with plenty of freshly ground black pepper and garnish with chopped parsley.

Top: *Pizza with Fisherman's Topping*
Bottom: *Roman-style Pizza (page 145)*

PIZZELLE – FRIED PIZZAS

Pizzelle are a traditional Neapolitan dish, usually made for a large gathering, to the delight of the children. They are traditionally served topped with sauce and stacked in piles which, when they arrive at the table, are quickly devoured. They keep their crispness better, however, if taken to the table before adding the sauce, which can be served separately in sauce boats. Two or three different toppings can then be prepared and everyone can choose his or her favourite one, finishing the meal by dipping one or two pizzas in caster sugar and thus making a dessert, too.

They are best eaten with your fingers!

PIZZELLE DOUGH

450 g/1 lb strong plain flour
1 teaspoon salt
25 g/1 oz fresh yeast
about 375 ml/13 fl oz tepid water
oil for deep frying

Sieve the flour and salt into a large mixing bowl and make a well in the centre. Dissolve the yeast in part of the tepid water and pour it into the well with the rest of the water. Mix the ingredients together to form a soft, fairly sticky dough.

Turn the dough out on to a well floured working surface and knead for approximately 10 minutes, until it becomes smooth and elastic. Add a little more flour if necessary until the dough stops sticking to your hand. Divide the dough into 16 pieces and knead each one into a ball.

Put the balls of dough on to a floured tray, cover and leave to rise for about 1 hour in a warm kitchen, until they have doubled in size.

Heat the oil for deep frying, checking that it is the correct temperature before using by dropping in a cube of bread. When the bread starts to fry, the oil is ready for use.

Fry the pizzas one or two at a time, depending on the size of the pan. Before dropping them into the oil, pull and flatten the balls into circles of approximately 13 cm/5 in. in diameter. The pizzas will float on the top of the oil, so when the underside is golden, turn them over and brown the other side.

Drain the pizzas well on kitchen paper and stack them into a pile, keeping them warm in the oven.

Serve immediately with your favourite sauce.

COOK'S TIP
Pizzelle are best cooked and eaten a few at a time so that they retain their crispness. When they are kept warm for any length of time the dough tends to become tough. These quantities make 16 pizzas of about 13 cm/5 in. in diameter. The usual serving is four pizzas per person.

TOPPINGS FOR PIZZELLE

SUGAR AND PEPPER TOPPING

(ZUCCHERO E PEPE)

1 quantity Pizzelle Dough (this page)
caster sugar
freshly ground black pepper

Sprinkle each pizza with caster sugar and freshly ground black pepper. The result will be sweet and spicy.

TOMATO AND BASIL SALAD TOPPING

800 g/1¾ lb ripe tomatoes
1 clove garlic
small bunch of fresh basil
salt
olive oil
1 quantity Pizzelle Dough (page 148)

Peel the tomatoes and remove the seeds. Roughly chop the pulp into small pieces. Peel and crush the clove of garlic and add it to the tomatoes. Wash, dry and tear the basil leaves into small pieces and add them to the tomatoes. Add salt to taste and a little olive oil. Mix the ingredients together well and cool in the refrigerator.

Top each pizza with a tablespoon of the tomato salad.

TOMATO AND BASIL TOPPING

(POMODORO E BASILICO)

575 g/1¼ lb canned tomatoes
3 cloves garlic
small bunch of fresh basil
olive oil
salt
65 g/2½ oz Parmesan cheese, grated
1 quantity Pizzelle Dough (page 148)

Crush the tomatoes or blend them briefly in a liquidiser. Peel and cut each clove of garlic into three or four pieces. Wash, dry and tear the basil leaves into small pieces.

Coat the bottom of the frying pan with olive oil. When the oil is hot, but not smoking, add the garlic and fry gently until golden. Add the tomatoes, the basil and salt to taste and simmer gently for approximately 15 minutes, until the sauce becomes denser.

Top each pizza with 1 or 2 tablespoons of sauce and sprinkle with grated Parmesan.

TOMATO AND OREGANO TOPPING

(POMODORO E ORIGANO)

575 g/1¼ lb canned tomatoes
3 cloves garlic
olive oil
salt
1 quantity Pizzelle Dough (page 148)
crushed oregano

Crush the tomatoes or blend them briefly in a liquidiser. Peel and cut each clove of garlic into three or four pieces.

Coat the bottom of the frying pan with olive oil. When the oil is hot, but not smoking, gently fry the garlic until golden. Add the tomatoes and salt to taste and simmer gently for approximately 15 minutes, until the sauce becomes denser.

Top each pizza with 1 or 2 tablespoons of sauce and sprinkle with crushed oregano.

COOK'S TIP
Olives and capers can be added to this sauce if desired.

OIL AND PARMESAN CHEESE TOPPING

(OLIO E PARMIGIANO)

1 quantity Pizzelle Dough (page 148)
65 g/2½ oz Parmesan cheese, grated
olive oil

Top each pizza with grated cheese and pour a little olive oil on top. A little chopped basil can be added if desired.

STUFFED PIZZAS AND SAVOURY CAKES

CALZONI

Illustrated opposite

POTATO DOUGH
1 (150-g/5-oz) potato
400 g/14 oz strong plain flour
plus extra for working the dough
1 teaspoon salt
25 g/1 oz fresh yeast
350 ml/12 fl oz tepid water

FILLING
100 g/4 oz lean cooked ham
225 g/8 oz mozzarella cheese
225 g/8 oz ricotta cheese
1 teaspoon chopped fresh basil
2 eggs
salt and freshly ground black pepper

Prepare the dough as for pizzas and leave to rise.

Trim the fat off the cooked ham and cut the meat into small pieces of approximately 1 cm/½ in. Cut the mozzarella into cubes of about 1 cm/½ in. Mix all the ingredients together with the two beaten eggs and add salt and freshly ground black pepper to taste.

When the dough has doubled in size, after about 1 hour, divide it into eight pieces and press each one out into a circle, approximately 15 cm/6 in. in diameter, picking the circles up and slapping them down on to the table as you would when making a pizza. Divide the filling into eight parts, putting it into the middle of each circle of dough. Moisten the edges of the circles with a little water and fold each one over to form a semi-circle, pressing the edges down well and sealing them in the same way as you would a savoury pie or pastry. Brush the calzoni with a little beaten egg.

Bake at the top of a very hot oven (240 C, 475 F, gas 9) for approximately 25 minutes, until they are well risen and golden brown.

COOK'S TIP
Calzoni can be fried instead of baked in the oven. Omit the egg glazing and fry in hot, deep oil for approximately 4–5 minutes on each side. Drain the calzoni well on kitchen paper and serve immediately. Fried calzoni are softer and lighter than the baked variety as they do not form a crust.

ALTERNATIVE FILLING FOR CALZONI

175 g/6 oz salami (in one piece)
225 g/8 oz mozzarella cheese
225 g/8 oz ricotta cheese
2 eggs
salt and freshly ground black pepper

Cut the salami into small pieces of about 5 mm/¼ in and follow the preceding calzoni recipe.

COOK'S TIP
Luncheon meat or spam can be substituted for the salami if preferred.

Top: *Savoury Easter Pizza Cake (page 160)*
Bottom: *Calzoni*

PIZZA FILLED WITH RICOTTA AND SPINACH

(PIZZA IMBOTTITA CON RICOTTA E SPINACI)

POTATO DOUGH
1 (150-g/5-oz) potato
400 g/14 oz strong plain flour
1 teaspoon salt
25 g/1 oz fresh yeast
350 ml/12 fl oz tepid water

FILLING
350 g/12 oz frozen whole-leaf spinach
225 g/8 oz ricotta cheese
2 eggs, beaten
50 g/2 oz Parmesan cheese, grated
½ teaspoon grated nutmeg
salt and freshly ground black pepper

Make the dough as for a normal pizza, divide it into two parts and leave it to rise until it has doubled in size.

Cook the spinach in boiling salted water and drain it well, squeezing out as much water as possible. Finely chop the spinach or blend it in a liquidiser and mix it with the ricotta, eggs, cheese, nutmeg and salt and pepper.

Press out two circles of dough approximately 25–30 cm/10–12 in. in diameter, in the same way as you would for a normal pizza. Make one of the circles slightly larger than the other. Place the larger circle on a greased baking tray.

Spread the filling over the dough, leaving a 2.5-cm/1-in border. Dampen the border with a little water. Place the other circle of dough on top of the first and seal the edges by folding the border of the bottom circle up over the one on top, pinching the two together. Make two or three small holes in the top of the pizza with a fine knitting needle or cocktail stick. Leave the pizza to rise for about 30 minutes before baking.

Bake at the top of a very hot oven (240 C, 475 F, gas 9) for approximately 30 minutes, until the pizza has risen well and is golden brown.

Serve the pizza hot and cut into slices.

COOK'S TIP
Any bitter, green vegetable can be used instead of spinach, for example endive. In this case a little chilli can be added when frying the garlic.

SPLIT PIZZA

(PIZZA SPACCATA)

DOUGH

300 g/11 oz strong plain flour
1 teaspoon salt
25 g/1 oz fresh yeast
4 tablespoons tepid water
2 eggs, beaten
2 tablespoons grated Parmesan cheese
100 g/4 oz margarine, softened

FILLING AND TOPPING

575 g/1$\frac{1}{4}$ lb canned tomatoes
1 small onion
olive oil
salt and pepper
small bunch of fresh basil
400 g/14 oz mozzarella cheese
2 tablespoons grated Parmesan cheese

Sieve the flour and salt into a mixing bowl and make a well in the centre. Dissolve the yeast in part of the tepid water and pour it into the well, together with the beaten eggs, grated cheese, remaining water and softened margarine. Mix all the ingredients together to form a very soft dough.

Turn the dough out on to a well-floured working surface and knead it for about 10 minutes until it becomes less sticky, and is smooth and elastic. Put the dough into a greased baking tin (approximately 25 cm/10 in. in diameter), press it down flat and leave it to rise, covered, until it has doubled in size. This will take about 2 hours.

Put the pizza in a moderate oven (180C, 350F, gas 4), as you light it. Bake for about 45 minutes, until it has risen well and is golden brown. Turn the pizza out of the tin and leave to cool.

Crush the tomatoes or blend them briefly in a liquidiser. Finely chop the onion. Coat the bottom of a large saucepan with oil and fry the onion gently until it is transparent. Add the tomatoes and salt to taste and simmer gently for approximately 15 minutes, until the sauce becomes denser.

Tear the basil leaves into small pieces and add them to the sauce at the last minute. Cut the mozzarella cheese into very thin slices.

When the pizza has cooled, cut it into two and take off the top half. Spread half the sauce on the lower half of the pizza and cover with slices of mozzarella cheese. Cover the bottom half with the top half and spread it with the rest of the sauce, cover with slices of mozzarella and sprinkle with grated Parmesan.

Bake the pizza in a moderately hot oven (200C, 400F, gas 6) for approximately 15 minutes, until it has heated through and the cheese has melted.

COOK'S TIP

The pizza can be made the day before and be split and filled just before serving.

PIZZA FILLED WITH SPINACH, PINE KERNELS AND SULTANAS

(PIZZA IMBOTTITA CON SPINACI, UVA PASSA E PINOLI)

DOUGH
25 g/1 oz fresh yeast
250 ml/8 fl oz tepid water
400 g/14 oz strong plain flour
1 teaspoon salt

FILLING
450 g/1 lb frozen whole-leaf spinach
salt . 3 cloves garlic
olive oil
1 tablespoon pine kernels, or chopped almonds . 1 tablespoon sultanas

Make the dough as for a normal pizza, divide it into two parts and leave it to rise until it has doubled in size. Cook the spinach in boiling salted water and drain well. Peel and cut each clove of garlic into three or four pieces.

Coat the bottom of the frying pan with olive oil, and when the oil is hot, but not smoking, add the garlic and fry until golden, adding the pine kernels, followed by the sultanas. Add the spinach and sauté gently for about 5 minutes.

Press out two circles of dough approximately 25–30 cm/10–12 in. in diameter, in the same way as you would for a normal pizza. Make one of them slightly larger than the other. Put the larger circle on to a greased baking tray.

Place the filling on the circle of dough, leaving a 2.5-cm/1-in border. Dampen the border with a little water. Place the second circle of dough on top of the first and seal the edges by folding the border of the bottom circle up over the one on top, pinching the two together. Make two or three small holes in the top of the pizza with a cocktail stick to allow the steam to escape. Leave the pizza to rise for 30 minutes before baking.

Bake in a very hot oven (240 C, 475 F, gas 9) for about 30 minutes until it is well risen and golden.

Top: *Double-decker Pizza (page 156)*
Bottom: *Savoury Pizza Ring (page 158)*

DOUBLE-DECKER PIZZA

(PIZZA A DUE STRATI)

Illustrated on pages 154 and 155

POTATO DOUGH

1 (150-g/5-oz) potato
400 g/14 oz strong plain flour
1 teaspoon salt
25 g/1 oz fresh yeast
350 ml/12 fl oz tepid water

FILLING AND TOPPING

4 hard-boiled eggs
150 g/5 oz lean cooked ham
225 g/8 oz mozzarella cheese
225 g/8 oz canned or fresh tomatoes
salt and freshly ground black pepper
$\frac{1}{2}$ teaspoon crushed oregano
1 tablespoon olive oil

Make the dough as for a normal pizza, divide it into two parts and leave it to rise until it has doubled in size.

Cut the hard-boiled eggs into wedges and chop the cooked ham and mozzarella into small pieces. Crush or slice the tomatoes.

Press the dough out into two circles about 25–30 cm/10–12 in. in diameter, in the same way as you would a normal pizza, making one of them slightly larger than the other. Place the larger one on a greased baking tray.

Put the chopped ham and mozzarella on to the pizza, leaving a border of approximately 1.5 cm/$\frac{3}{4}$ in. Arrange the wedges of hard-boiled egg on top, sprinkle with a little salt and plenty of freshly ground black pepper. Dampen the border with a little water.

Cover the pizza with the second circle of dough and seal the edges well, folding the border of the bottom circle up over the top one and pinching them well together. Make one or two small holes in the top with a cocktail stick to allow the steam to escape. Leave the pizza to rise for about 30 minutes.

Spread the tomatoes over the top, sprinkle with oregano and a little salt and pour on the olive oil.

Bake at the top of a very hot oven (240 C, 475 F, gas 9) for approximately 25 minutes, until the pizza has risen well and the border is golden.

Serve the pizza hot, in slices.

COOK'S TIP

Different fillings can be invented and olives can be added.

Easter Pizza

(Pizza di Pasqua)

DOUGH

450 g/1 lb strong plain flour
$\frac{1}{2}$ teaspoon salt
25 g/1 oz fresh yeast
300 ml/$\frac{1}{2}$ pint tepid water
50 g/2 oz lard, flaked
50 g/2 oz Parmesan cheese, grated
freshly ground black pepper

FILLING

175 g/6 oz salami
75 g/3 oz Emmental cheese
75 g/3 oz Provolone cheese
6 eggs
25 g/1 oz pecorino cheese, grated
salt and freshly ground black pepper

Sieve the flour and salt into a mixing bowl and make a well in the centre. Dissolve the yeast in the tepid water and pour it into the well. Add the lard, grated cheese and plenty of freshly ground black pepper.

Mix the ingredients together into a soft dough, turn it out on to a floured working surface and knead for approximately 10 minutes, slapping it down vigorously on to the table occasionally. Knead the dough until it becomes smooth and elastic, adding a little more flour if necessary to stop it from sticking. Put the dough into a floured bowl, cover and leave to rise for about 1$\frac{1}{2}$ hours until it has doubled in size.

Cut the salami and cheeses into small pieces of approximately 5 mm/$\frac{1}{4}$ in. Beat the eggs well, adding the grated cheese and salt and pepper to taste. Add half the salami and diced cheeses.

When the dough has risen sufficiently, knock it back and divide it into two parts of about one-third and two-thirds. Using the larger piece, work it out into a circle large enough to line a baking tin approximately 23 cm/9 in. in diameter. Work the smaller piece into a circle large enough to make a lid for the pie.

Grease the baking tin and line it with the dough. Put the rest of the chopped cheeses and salami into the tin and press them down gently into the dough. Pour in the egg mixture. Moisten the edges of the lid and place it over the filling, sealing the edges well to make sure that the egg mixture will not escape. Make a few small holes in the top with a cocktail stick, to allow the steam to escape. Leave to rise for approximately 1$\frac{1}{2}$ hours before baking.

Bake in the middle of a very hot oven (240 C, 475 F, gas 9) for about 45 minutes, until the pizza has risen well and is golden brown.

COOK'S TIP

This pizza is best served tepid, or even cold. It is ideal for parties or picnics. In Naples they make this pizza at Easter to offer to unexpected guests who may call round with their Easter greetings.

SAVOURY PIZZA RING

(TORTANO)

Illustrated on pages 154 and 155

DOUGH

200 g/7 oz strong plain flour
½ teaspoon salt
20 g/¾ oz fresh yeast
7 tablespoons tepid water
50 g/2 oz lard
40 g/1½ oz Parmesan cheese, grated
freshly ground black pepper

FILLING

40 g/1½ oz Emmental or Gruyère cheese
65 g/2½ oz mozzarella cheese
40 g/1½ oz Provolone cheese
65 g/2½ oz salami
2 portions cheese spread
2 hard-boiled eggs

Sieve the flour and salt into a bowl and make a well in the centre. Dissolve the yeast in the tepid water and pour it into the well. Add the lard, grated cheese and plenty of freshly ground black pepper.

Mix the ingredients together to form a soft dough, turn it out on to a floured working surface and knead it for about 10 minutes, slapping it down vigorously on to the table occasionally. Knead until the dough becomes smooth and elastic, adding a little more flour if necessary to stop it from sticking.

Put the dough into a floured bowl, cover and leave to rise for approximately 1½ hours until the dough has doubled in size.

Cut the three cheeses and the salami into small pieces of approximately 5 mm/¼ in and mix them together with the cheese spread. Cut each hard-boiled egg into six wedges.

When the dough has risen, knock it back and work it out into a rectangle on a floured working surface, until it is about the length needed to form a ring in the baking tin. Cover the surface with the chopped cheeses and salami and arrange the wedges of hard-boiled egg in rows lengthways. Roll the dough up as tightly as possible, to form a long sausage shape and seal the open edge of the dough to prevent the filling from escaping.

Grease a ring-shaped baking tin (approximately 23 cm/9 in. in diameter) and put the dough into it, forming a ring. Pinch the two ends of the roll together well to seal in the filling. Leave the dough to rise for another 1½–2 hours, covered with a tea-towel, until it has doubled in size.

Bake in the middle of a moderately hot oven (200 C, 400 F, gas 6) for approximately 45 minutes, until the ring has risen well and has turned golden.

The pizza ring should be served cold, but is best eaten the same day.

COOK'S TIP

This is a traditional Neapolitan recipe which uses up leftover pieces of cheese and salami, so you can substitute a variety of leftovers for the given ingredients. It is ideal for parties, picnics or served with a glass of cool, white wine.

MERINGUED PIZZA WITH ARTICHOKES

(PIZZA MERINGATA DI CARCIOFI)

DOUGH

25 g/1 oz fresh yeast
250 ml/8 fl oz tepid water
400 g/14 oz strong plain flour
1 teaspoon salt
40 g/1½ oz margarine, softened

FILLING

4 globe artichokes
juice of ½ lemon
50 g/2 oz butter
1 spicy Italian sausage, skinned and crumbled
3 eggs
2 tablespoons Binding White Sauce (page 99)
salt and freshly ground black pepper

Make the dough as for a normal pizza, adding the margarine when adding the other ingredients to the flour. Leave the dough to rise until it has doubled in size.

Prepare the artichokes by pulling off the tough outside leaves until those underneath are whitish. Cut off the top third of the artichokes to eliminate the tips of the leaves. Peel the stalks, leaving the tender core. Rub the prepared artichokes with lemon juice and leave them in cold water and lemon juice for approximately 15 minutes. Drain them well and cut them lengthways into thin wedges and the stalks into thin strips.

Fry the artichokes gently in the butter and add the sausage. Separate the eggs and beat the yolks into the white sauce. Add the sauce to the artichokes and sausage in the frying pan. Stir the mixture well. Add salt and freshly ground black pepper to taste.

Line a greased baking tin or flan dish (about 30 cm/12 in. in diameter) with the dough. Pour the filling into the centre of the dough and spread it out evenly. Whisk the whites of the eggs until they are stiff and cover the filled pizza with them, sealing the meringue on to the border of the pizza.

Bake in the middle of a moderately hot oven (200 C, 400 F, gas 6) for approximately 30 minutes, until the pizza has risen well and the top is golden.

COOK'S TIP

Do not be disappointed when the meringue is neither white nor crisp; remember that it is savoury and not sweet. It simply acts as a lid to the filling.

SAVOURY EASTER PIZZA CAKE

(CASATIELLO)

Illustrated on page 151

400 g/14 oz strong plain flour
1 teaspoon salt
150 g/5 oz lard
40 g/1½ oz fresh yeast
about 250 ml/8 fl oz tepid water
25 g/1 oz Parmesan cheese, grated
20 g/¾ oz pecorino cheese, grated
freshly ground black pepper
4 fresh eggs plus a little beaten egg to glaze

Sieve the flour and salt into a mixing bowl, make a well in the centre and add approximately one-fifth of the lard. Dissolve the yeast in part of the tepid water and add it, with the rest of the water, to the flour and lard in the bowl. Mix the ingredients together to form a soft dough. Turn the dough out on to a floured working surface and knead it for approximately 10 minutes, until it becomes smooth and elastic. Put it into a floured bowl, cover and leave to rise for about 1½ hours until it has doubled in size.

Turn the dough out on to a floured working surface and press it out into a rectangle about 1 cm/½ in thick. Spread lard over the surface, sprinkle with the mixed grated cheese and lots of freshly ground black pepper and fold the rectangle over. Seal the edges and repeat the process. Push the dough out again with your hands into a rectangle the same size as the first and repeat the operation twice more. Push the dough out into a rectangle again, spread it with the last of the lard, sprinkle with the last of the cheese and pepper and roll the dough up into a long sausage shape.

Cut off a small portion of dough from the end of the roll and knead it into a small ball the size of a bread roll. Put the long roll of dough into a greased ring-shaped baking tin (approximately 23 cm/9 in. in diameter) and pinch the open ends together to form a ring. Cover and leave to rise for about 3 hours. Put the small ball of dough into a floured bowl and leave it to rise with the ring of dough.

Gently scrub the four eggs to make sure that the shells are clean.

When the dough has doubled in size, roll the small ball out into a long, thin pencil-shaped strip and cut it into eight pieces. Place the eggs on top of the ring of dough with the pointed ends towards the centre of the ring. Secure each egg in place by forming a cross with two of the pieces of dough. Pinch the ends of the strips into the dough of the ring to make sure that they are firmly attached.

Bake in the centre of a moderate oven (180 C, 350 F, gas 4) for about 1 hour, glazing the surface with a little beaten egg 10 minutes before the pizza is ready. (The pizza must be put into a fairly cool oven, so light the oven just before fixing the eggs on top.)

Serve when cold, but Casatiello is best eaten the same day.

COOK'S TIP

This is a traditional Neapolitan recipe. Casatiello is served instead of bread to accompany salami, hard-boiled eggs and pickles, which form part of the Easter Sunday lunch. It is also offered to friends who happen to 'drop in' around Easter time and is delicious as a snack served with a glass of cool, white wine.

Savoury Pizza Cake

(Rustico)

**225 g/8 oz strong-flavoured cheese, such as
Cheddar or Emmental
225 g/8 oz salami
450 g/1 lb strong plain flour
1 teaspoon salt
50 g/2 oz fresh yeast
175 ml/6 fl oz tepid water
150 ml/$\frac{1}{4}$ pint corn oil**

Cut the cheese and salami into very small pieces of approximately 5 mm/$\frac{1}{4}$ in.

Sieve the flour and salt into a bowl and make a well in the centre. Blend the yeast with the tepid water and pour this into the well together with the oil. Mix the ingredients together to form a soft, sticky dough.

Add the chopped salami and cheese and mix thoroughly. Press the mixture into a greased baking tin about 30 cm/12 in. in diameter, cover with a tea-towel and leave to rise for about 2–2$\frac{1}{2}$ hours, until the dough has doubled in size.

Bake in the centre of a very hot oven (240 C, 475 F, gas 9) for approximately 30 minutes, until the pizza has risen well and is golden brown.

Serve warm or cold, but is best eaten the same day.

Cook's Tip

Different kinds of chopped ingredients can be added to the dough. Instead of salami, luncheon meat or cooked ham can be used. Chopped hard-boiled eggs can be added, too. The quantity of chopped ingredients can be varied according to taste.

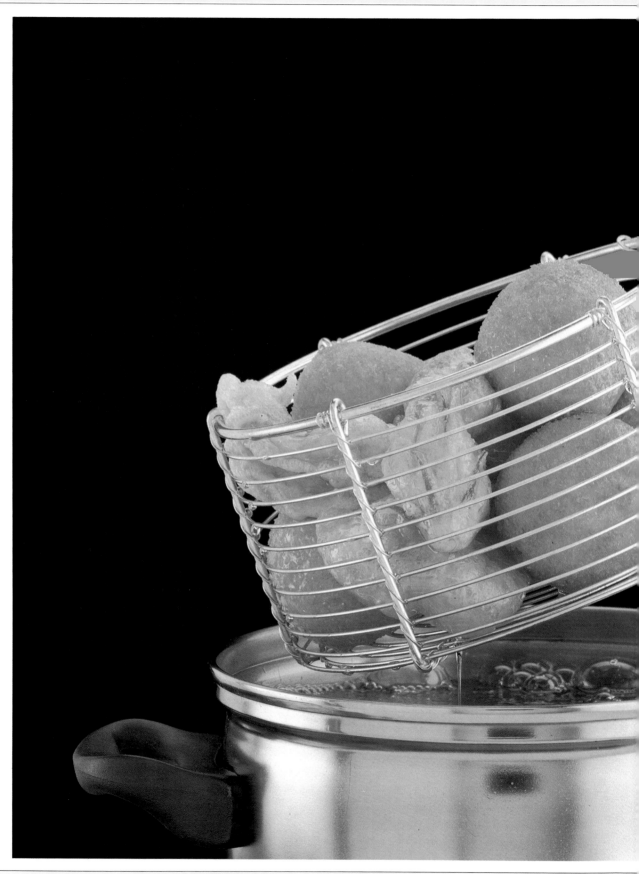

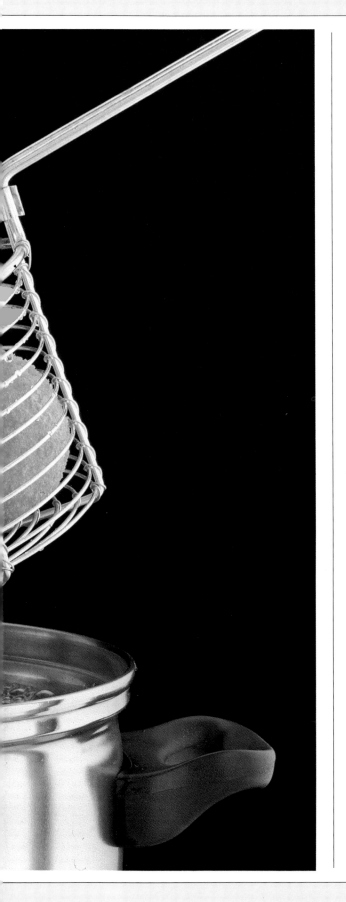

STARTERS AND FILLERS

The pizzerias in Italy make various tit-bits which are served either to stave off the pangs of hunger while you are waiting for your pizza to arrive, or eaten as a 'filler' if one pizza is not quite enough to satisfy your appetite but you do not really want another.

I decided to include these recipes as they are all very tasty snacks, which can be made in a few minutes to eat straight away or to freeze and bring out when you are making pizzas!

GARLIC BREAD

(BRUSCHETTA)

8 thick slices crusty bread
1 clove garlic, peeled
olive oil
salt

Toast the bread well on both sides and rub one side with the garlic. Place the slices of toast on a large serving plate and pour a little oil over them. Sprinkle with salt and serve while hot.

COOK'S TIP

Garlic bread is delicious served with slices of Parma ham or salami as a snack or as the starter to a meal. The bread should be as 'coarse' as possible, for example a farmhouse or wholemeal loaf.

Savoury Rice Balls (page 164) and Courgette Flowers (page 166)

POTATO CROQUETTES

(CROQUETTES DI PATATE)

**6 medium–large old potatoes
50 g/2 oz Parmesan cheese, grated
1 tablespoon finely chopped parsley
2 teaspoons grated lemon peel
2 eggs
salt
100 g/4 oz mozzarella cheese
beaten egg and breadcrumbs
oil for frying**

Scrub the potatoes well and boil them whole in their skins until soft (about 30–40 minutes). Drain the potatoes well and allow them to cool. When they are tepid, peel and mash them and put the mashed potato into a large mixing bowl.

Add the Parmesan, parsley, lemon peel, eggs and salt to taste and knead them into the potatoes until you get a smooth mixture. Cut the mozzarella cheese into 1 × 2.5-cm/½ × 1-in pieces.

Form the potato mixture into small rolls approximately 7.5 cm/3 in long and 2.5 cm/1 in across. Push a piece of mozzarella into the centre of each roll, cover it with potato and re-form the roll. Coat the croquettes with beaten egg and cover with breadcrumbs, 'squaring off' the ends of the rolls.

Fry the croquettes in hot oil until golden brown. Drain well on kitchen paper.

Serve while piping hot.

COOK'S TIP
The mozzarella cheese can be omitted if preferred.

The croquettes are best deep fried, but shallow oil can be used if necessary.

These quantities make 20 croquettes.

SAVOURY RICE BALLS

(SUPPLÌ)

Illustrated on pages 162 and 163

**350 g/12 oz rice
2 ladles Ragoût Sauce (page 57)
50 g/2 oz small frozen peas
25 g/1 oz Parmesan cheese, grated
100 g/4 oz mozzarella cheese
salt
beaten egg and breadcrumbs
oil for frying**

Cook the rice in the ragoût sauce, adding the peas and a little meat from the sauce, broken up into small pieces. Stirring frequently, keep adding a glass of water when the mixture gets too dense, until the rice is cooked. When ready, the rice should be tender and it should have absorbed all sauce. Add the Parmesan and mix well. Leave the rice to cool.

Cut the mozzarella into small lengths of about 2.5 cm/1 in × 1 cm/½ in. Shape the rice into small egg-shaped balls, pushing a piece of mozzarella cheese into the centre of each one. The supplì should be roughly the size of a medium egg. Coat the balls with beaten egg and cover with breadcrumbs.

Fry the supplì in hot oil until golden brown. They are best deep fried. Drain well on kitchen paper.

Serve the supplì while piping hot.

COOK'S TIP
The mozzarella cheese melts when cooked and when the supplì is broken in two and pulled apart, the cheese forms a long filament, or 'wire', which joins the two halves. For this reason the supplì are called *al telefono* which means 'like a telephone'. These quantities make 16 supplì.

TOASTS
(CROSTINI)

350 g/12 oz mozzarella cheese
12 slices French bread
olive oil
4 slices Parma ham

Cut the mozzarella cheese into 12 thin slices. Cover each slice of bread with a slice of cheese and put on a greased baking tray in groups of three, the slices overlapping each other slightly. Pour a little olive oil over the top and place a slice of Parma ham on top of each group of slices.

Bake in a very hot oven (240 C, 475 F, gas 9) for about 15 minutes, until the bread is crisp and the cheese has melted. Serve immediately.

COOK'S TIP
A spreading of anchovy paste or crushed anchovy fillets may be substituted for the ham. The crostini are best baked and served on individual ovenproof plates or dishes.

FAKE PIZZA

1 clove garlic
1 (227-g/8-oz) can tomatoes
4 large thick slices crusty bread
salt
crushed oregano
olive oil

Crush the tomatoes or blend them briefly in a liquidiser. Crush the garlic and mix it with the tomatoes. Place the slices of bread on a baking tray and spread them with the tomato mixture. Sprinkle with salt and oregano and pour a little olive oil on top.

Bake in the middle of a moderately hot oven (200 C, 400 F, gas 6) for approximately 15–20 minutes.

COOK'S TIP
Mozzarella cheese and fresh basil can be substituted for the dried oregano if preferred.

COURGETTE FLOWERS

(FIORI DI ZUCCHINI)

16 courgette flowers
75 g/3 oz plain flour
salt
oil for frying

Very gently rinse the flowers under running water, opening the petals to make sure that there are no insects or foreign bodies hidden inside. Gently pat the flowers dry with kitchen paper and cut off the stalks. Flatten the flowers slightly by pressing them at the base.

Add just enough cold water to the flour to make a thickish batter and stir well to remove any lumps, adding a pinch of salt. Coat the flowers with the batter.

Fry in hot oil until crisp and golden.

Serve the courgette flowers while piping hot.

COOK'S TIP

The flowers can also be stuffed with a cube of mozzarella cheese and a small piece of anchovy fillet. The tips of the petals should then be twisted together before coating the flowers with the batter. Some people prefer to add yeast to the batter.

MOZZARELLA IN COACHES

(MOZZARELLA IN CARROZZA)

8 small slices stale bread
2 eggs
salt
225 g/8 oz mozzarella cheese
milk
oil for frying

Cut the crusts off the slices of bread. Beat the eggs well, adding salt to taste. Cut the mozzarella into enough slices to cover four of the slices of bread. Dip the bread into the milk and make four sandwiches with the bread and mozzarella cheese. Coat the sandwiches with the beaten egg, allowing the egg to soak well into the bread.

Fry the sandwiches in hot oil until golden brown on both sides.

Serve immediately while piping hot.

COOK'S TIP

Different shapes can be cut out of the mozzarella sandwiches, before frying, using pastry cutters. These will amuse children or will look good at parties. The shapes can be coated in breadcrumbs after being dipped in the egg, if preferred.

BATTER BALLS OR SAVOURY DOUGHNUTS

(PASTE CRESCIUTE)

350 g/12 oz strong plain flour
1 teaspoon salt
25 g/1 oz fresh yeast
450 ml/$\frac{3}{4}$ pint tepid water
2 (50-g/2-oz) cans anchovy fillets
oil for deep frying

Sieve the flour and salt into a mixing bowl and make a well in the centre. Blend the yeast with 150 ml/$\frac{1}{4}$ pint of the tepid water and pour it into the well. Using a fork, start beating the flour into the liquid, adding the remaining tepid water until all the flour has been incorporated and you have a very thick batter. Cover the bowl and leave the batter to rise for about 1–1$\frac{1}{2}$ hours, until it has doubled in size.

Rinse the anchovy fillets under running water and pat them dry on kitchen paper, breaking them into small pieces of approximately 1 cm/$\frac{1}{2}$ in.

Heat the oil for deep frying, checking that it is the correct temperature before using by dropping in a cube of bread. When the bread starts to fry, the oil is ready for use.

Drop a few pieces of anchovy fillet on to the surface of the batter. Take spoonfuls of batter, with a few pieces of anchovy in each, and drop them into the hot oil. Fry them until golden. Continue in this way until you have used up all the batter. The number of balls will depend on the size of the spoon used. The normal size is a scant tablespoon, but mini-balls can be made for parties.

Drain the batter balls well on kitchen paper and sprinkle them with a little salt.

Serve immediately, piping hot.

COOK'S TIP

Different ingredients can be used to flavour the balls, for example, small cubes of cheese, (add a little grated cheese to the batter, too) courgette flowers, small pieces of salami. The traditional filling is, however, anchovies.

GLOSSARY

Al dente:
a term used to describe properly cooked pasta, *al dente* means 'resistant to the tooth'. Two or three minutes before the end of the recommended cooking time, test the pasta. It is perfectly cooked when the uncooked core in the centre is just about to disappear or, in the case of spaghetti, when you can squeeze it between thumb and forefinger to break it.

Basil *(sweet basil and bush basil):*
a herb used extensively in Italian cooking, basil is a perfect complement to tomatoes and mozzarella cheese in particular. It forms the basis of the famous pasta sauce, Pesto Genovese (see the recipe on page 42). Basil can be used fresh or dried, and is easily obtained from supermarkets in its dried form. But the flavour of fresh basil is superior, and also easily obtained, since basil is an ideal herb to grow in pots and window boxes; grow it indoors on a window sill in winter, and outdoors in summer. Sweet basil grows to about 45 cm/18 in, while bush basil grows to about half that height and has smaller leaves.

Boletus mushrooms:
fragrant yellow mushrooms found in conifer woods, but, more safely, bought dried in small packets in some delicatessens. Substitute field mushrooms or any mushroom with a strong flavour if boletus are not available.

Cannellini beans:
small, plump white haricot beans. Commonly available dried or canned. The dried variety requires lengthy soaking before cooking.

Capers:
these small flower buds from a Mediterranean shrub are sold pickled in small jars. They are dull green in colour and have a piquant flavour. Capers are found in many supermarkets and delicatessens.

Chillies:
hot peppers which can be bought fresh or dried in many big supermarkets, greengrocers' and specialist stores. They come in various shapes, colours and sizes. Plump green chillies are among the mildest. Both the seeds and the case of chillies are hot and should be handled with care. Read the note on page 40 before preparing them.

Courgette flowers:
if you grow courgettes in the garden, you will be familiar with their sizeable flowers, but you may not have prepared them, Italian-style, dipped in batter and deep fried. See the recipe for doing so on page 166.

Fennel seeds:
dried seeds of the Mediterranean herb, which was introduced to England by the Romans. Fennel grows to about four feet tall and has feathery leaves and many small clusters of flowers. The seeds have an aniseed flavour.

Fontina cheese:
a fairly hard cheese with a few little holes, from Italy's Piedmont region. It is rather like the Swiss Gruyère cheese in texture, and similarly melts well.

Garlic:
the most pungent member of the onion family, garlic is a bulb made up of lots of small bulbs, called cloves. Garlic is celebrated as a medicinal herb in many countries, but most of all as a culinary seasoning. It is sold singly, in little nets, or in strings. Look for plump, firm bulbs when selecting garlic.

Gorgonzola cheese:
a famous blue cheese from Italy, moister than the famous English blue cheese, Stilton, Gorgonzola is creamy in texture and has a particularly strong flavour. This is produced by *penicillium gorgonzola*, which creates the blue veining.

Italian-style spicy sausages:
these highly seasoned fresh pork sausages are flavoured with pepper. Unlike many English sausages, no breadcrumbs are added to the meat. These sausages are available in Italian delicatessens.

Marjoram *(sweet, or cultivated):*
a native of the Mediterranean, sweet marjoram grows best in a warm climate, and is damaged by frost. But it can be grown in your own garden if sown each year. Marjoram is especially good used fresh with lamb, stuffings and potato dishes. Dried marjoram is excellent in tomato sauces, giving quite a strong, herby flavour.

Mozzarella cheese:
a slightly rubbery, soft and mild-tasting cheese, mozzarella is excellent served sliced with freshly ground black pepper, fresh basil and olive oil as an *hors d'oeuvre*, as well as in pizza toppings and calzoni. Once made exclusively from buffalo milk, it is now made

from cows' milk. Mozzarella will keep fresh for a few days if stored in a bowl of water in the refrigerator. **Provola** is a smoked version of mozzarella, with a brown skin which must be peeled off before use.

Olive oil:

the indispensable accompaniment to salads, pasta sauces and a multitude of Mediterranean dishes, virgin oil is the best and most expensive form in which olive oil can be bought. It comes from the first cold pressing of fresh, ripe olives. Aficionados will try to bring back a can from the country of source after a Mediterranean holiday, which is cheaper than buying virgin oil imported into England. The contents of cans and bottles labelled 'pure olive oil' are from subsequent pressings and a lower grade of olive.

Olives:

anyone who has been on holiday to the Mediterranean will have admired the groves of gnarled olive trees with silvery leaves and perhaps have seen olives being harvested. The difference between green and black olives is that the black ones are ripe. Green olives are picked young and soaked in brine to develop their colour and take away the bitter flavour. Black olives have had time to ripen on the tree and develop more oil before going to the presses. Black olives for eating are preserved in oil or brine and vary from plump, succulent specimens to tiny wrinkled editions. They frequently form part of pizza toppings in Italy. Buy olives loose from good delicatessens, or bottled from supermarkets. You can sometimes sample olives before buying them in delicatessens. Store those you do not eat in a jar of olive oil in the refrigerator.

Oregano *(wild marjoram)*:

like marjoram, oregano is widely used in tomato dishes. It is very popular in Italy and frequently used dried in pizza toppings and pasta sauces which include cheese and tomatoes. Oregano also complements the flavours of aubergines and courgettes and has a pronounced, aromatic flavour.

Parma ham:

a delicately flavoured and expensive uncooked ham, cured at Parma in Italy. It is eaten in transparently fine slices when used as an *hors d'oeuvre*, and traditionally served with melon.

Parmesan cheese:

to pasta lovers, probably the best known Italian cheese, as it is sprinkled liberally over so many pasta sauces and soups. It is a very hard, grainy cheese, most often found ready grated, in packets or cartons. If you can buy it fresh instead of grated, and grate it just before use, the flavour will be superior. A coarse rotary grater is the best one to use. Parmesan can also be frozen and used straight from the freezer.

Pecorino cheese:

like Parmesan, pecorino is a very hard, grainy cheese, which is used in the same way as Parmesan. Unlike Parmesan, which is made from cows' milk, pecorino is made from sheep's milk.

Pine kernels:

seeds of the stone pine, a tree native to the Mediterranean, pine kernels are small, pale and oval, resembling very small, blanched almonds. They are available in small packets and although expensive to buy, they are not often an essential ingredient and therefore go a long way.

Provolone cheese:

a fairly hard, smoked cheese, which is sold in a variety of shapes, including cylindrical and dumpy pear shape. Provolones are hung by cords to mature and you sometimes have to duck to avoid bumping into them hanging up in low-ceilinged Italian delicatessens.

Ricotta cheese:

a soft cheese which is lighter in flavour and texture than cream cheese, but not tangy like curd cheese. Ricotta is frequently used in cooked dishes, for example to fill pasta such as ravioli (see the recipe on page 32) and it does not melt during cooking. It is available from delicatessens or good delicatessen counters in supermarkets.

Salami:

a type of highly seasoned, preserved Italian sausage. Salamis are made of uncooked meat, usually a mixture of lean pork, pork fat and beef, and flavoured with wine, peppercorns, garlic or spices. The sausages are left to mature in brine, during which time they loose moisture and become dried. Some are smoked as a form of preservation. Each region has its own traditional type of salami, so there are infinite varieties to sample.

Squid:

a bizarre-looking sea creature, similar in appearance to an octopus. To prepare it, pull the head and tentacles away from the body and remove the mottled skin from the body. Remove the transparent cartilage from inside the squid, wash the squid and remove the two flaps from the body. Cut the tentacles away from the head, remove the ink sac – which can be reserved for use in an accompanying sauce – and discard the head. Slice the body into rings, the flaps into strips and the tentacles into bite-sized pieces. Squid can be cooked for a very short or a very long time; it will otherwise be very tough.

INDEX